Mary Douglas, now Director of Research at the
Russell Sage Foundation, New York, was Professor
of Anthropology at University College London from
1970 until 1977. She is the author of *The Lele of the
Kasai, Purity and Danger, Natural Symbols, Implicit
Meanings* and, most recently, *The World of Goods*.

Modern Masters

ARTAUD	Martin Esslin
BECKETT	A. Alvarez
CAMUS	Conor Cruise O'Brien
CHOMSKY	John Lyons
DURKHEIM	Anthony Giddens
EINSTEIN	Jeremy Bernstein
ELIOT	Stephen Spender
ENGELS	David McLellan
EVANS-PRITCHARD	Mary Douglas
FREUD	Richard Wollheim
GRAMSCI	James Joll
HEIDEGGER	George Steiner
JOYCE	John Gross
JUNG	Anthony Storr
KAFKA	Erich Heller
KLEIN	Hanna Segal
LAWRENCE	Frank Kermode
LE CORBUSIER	Stephen Gardiner
LENIN	Robert Conquest
LÉVI-STRAUSS	Edmund Leach
MARX	David McLellan
NIETZSCHE	J. P. Stern
ORWELL	Raymond Williams
PAVLOV	J. A. Gray
PIAGET	Margaret Boden
POPPER	Bryan Magee
POUND	Donald Davie
PROUST	Roger Shattuck
REICH	Charles Rycroft
RUSSELL	A. J. Ayer
SARTRE	Arthur C. Danto
SAUSSURE	Jonathan Culler
SCHOENBERG	Charles Rosen
TROTSKY	Irving Howe
WEBER	Donald MacRae
WITTGENSTEIN	David Pears
YEATS	Denis Donoghue

Evans-Pritchard

Mary Douglas

Fontana Paperbacks

First published by Fontana Paperbacks 1980
Copyright © Mary Douglas 1980

Set in Linotype Pilgrim

Made and printed in Great Britain by
William Collins Sons & Co. Ltd, Glasgow

A hardback edition of *Evans-Pritchard*
is published by Harvester Press

Contents

Acknowledgements 7
Biographical Note 9

1. Introduction 11
2. Human Mental Faculties 15
3. The Continuity of Evans-Pritchard's Programme 29
4. Fieldwork Methods 39
5. Accountability among the Azande 49
6. Accountability among the Nuer 62
7. Reasoning and Memory 74
8. Nuer Religion 87
9. Contradiction 107
10. Evans-Pritchard's Contemporary Influence 116

Notes 125
Short Bibliography 133

Acknowledgements

I thank the Russell Sage Foundation, New York, in whose employ I am, for allowing me time and resources for writing this book. Clearly it is a personal view. I am grateful to Christopher Ricks for criticizing that view. I thank Robert Merton for guidance on the development of the sociology of knowledge; Thomas Luckmann, P. Viazzo and Jeffrey Stout for discussion of *Nuer Religion*; Thomas Kuhn for correcting the account of feedback. T. O. Beidelman's *Bibliography of the Writings of E. E. Evans-Pritchard* (1974) has been invaluable. I am grateful to Denis Hynes for help with the bibliography and to Madeline Spitaleri for producing the finished manuscript.

Biographical Note

Born 1902, died 1973; married 1939 Ioma Heaton Nicholls (died 1959), five children; military service in Sudan and North Africa 1940–5; received into Roman Catholic Church 1944; with Meyer Fortes helped to found Association of Social Anthropologists 1946.

Education: Winchester College; Exeter College, Oxford; PhD. 1927 at London School of Economics.

Fieldwork, 1926–39: six major and several minor anthropological expeditions to Africa including Azande, twenty months, 1926–30; Nuer, twelve months, 1930–6; and Anuak, Shilluk and Nilotic Luo.

University Posts: 1923–31, Lecturer, London School of Economics. 1932–4, Professor of Sociology, Fuad I University (now Egyptian University of Cairo).

1935–40, Research Lecturer in African Sociology, University of Oxford.

1945, Reader in Anthropology, Cambridge University.

1946, Professor of Social Anthropology, University of Oxford.

1950, Visiting Professor of Anthropology, University of Chicago.

1957, Fellow, Center for Advanced Study in Behavioral Sciences, Stanford, University of California.

1. Introduction

'I should make it clear at this point that I am not, and never have been clever; imaginative and industrious if you like, but not clever in a bookish way of speaking ...'[1] So Sir Edward Evans-Pritchard in his old age described his own talents, knowing that he had achieved a resounding reputation in anthropology. The object of this book is to explain to readers unacquainted with this field what he did and why his thought is significant for the contemporary world of letters. He was a highly independent thinker who made signal advances in many branches of anthropology. His standing as a master of modern thought rests upon his solitary confronting, in the 1930s, of intellectual dilemmas that are now crowding in heavily upon the social sciences forty or fifty years later.

It is only right to say that this is not a straight summary, and something different from a synthesis. I have made a personal reconstruction upon the writings, forcing them into closer confrontation with problems that were evidently present to Evans-Pritchard but which have become more public and explicit since. There was no need to go beyond Evans-Pritchard to explain the importance of his work to specialists. The challenge here is to interest others in solutions to problems they have never considered before. While I was pondering how to focus, I realized that a name for his method was missing. A name is a powerful concentrator of ideas. By naming a theory of social accountability, I can show more cogently the methodological advances that can only be built upon his work. Thus his own intention of relating moral philosophy and religion systematically with social behaviour would be better fulfilled. The reader will have no difficulty, I hope, in distinguishing the master's original work from the pupil's presentation.

One of the present crises in sociology comes from the

criticisms of phenomenologists. Maintaining that social understanding must start from the human experience of consciousness and reflection, they despair of truth in any so-called humane science that ignores the distinctively human element. These critics have undermined confidence in the traditional methods and even in the traditional objectives of sociology. Consequently many scholars, sensitive to the criticism, have been tempted to give up striving for objectivity and to shift their own writing into a mystical mode, indulgent to their own subjectivity. Others, who would still like to try for objective comparisons, find little alternative but to work on in the old framework of enquiry, and so tend to shirk these issues. In advance of this critical juncture Evans-Pritchard felt the dilemma keenly. He would not subscribe to mechanistic social theories and resisted scientistic fashions in anthropology. His own rugged individualism forbade him to ignore individual human agency, and he found uncongenial any theorizing that reduced the mind to a mere arena in which social factors contend. It would go against his private philosophy to diminish persons in their autonomous personhood, even as objects of research, still more as objects of social engineering. But he did not abandon the wish for objective comparisons. So in his own work he met the problems that now beset us all more generally. He taught that the essential point for comparison is that at which people meet misfortune. They may accuse others, they may accept responsibility. They count different kinds of misfortune as needing explanation. As they work their ideas of blame and compensation into their social institutions, they invoke existences and powers that are adapted to each particular accounting system. There are ways of getting valid evidence on these essential moral purposes as they surface from consciousness into action.

The simplest formula in which to sum up these methods and the assumptions they rest upon is 'tracing accountability'. This book will argue that Evans-Pritchard's method of tracing notions of accountability through their institutional forms, because it starts with moral agents and their ideas about morality, shows a way out of the current difficulties in sociology. By tracing penalties and moral confrontations, a method of selecting and recording evidence emerges. The effort to classify kinds of accountability in different social systems requires a careful sifting of information. The method carries its own internal audit system. Theoretically, payments of debt and executions of justice, when they cover the whole of social life, should tally. If they do not, there is something more to research and explain. One of the strengths of the method is that it rests on the assumption that human society is composed not of cyphers, but of active agencies endowed with intelligence and will. Intentions create and sustain institutions as much as institutions constrain intentions. Starting from here the analysis opens upon questions not entertained in traditional sociology.

Another feature of his modernity is Evans-Pritchard's anticipation of the sociology of everyday knowledge. It has been respectable since the nineteenth century to research into the history of ideas and the sociology of knowledge. But these subjects have been venerably dressed in capital letters, as it were, and only recently has the artificial compartmentalizing of different branches of knowledge been criticized. The phenomenological writings of Husserl and Schutz have provoked a move to develop a systematic sociology of the commonsense knowledge of ordinary people in everyday contexts. Evans-Pritchard's specialized problem in anthropology led him early to that development because he could not deal with magic and totemism in specialized compartments. Furthermore, he extraordinarily anticipated the intentions of everyday-language philosophers by his recognition of the need to interpret speech fully in its context of functioning social relations and especially, of course, in social accounting.

(Another way in which Evans-Pritchard was in advance of his time may be no more than a curious byway of history : but he did analyse a negative feedback system in 1940. As the final abstraction from social reality, system was frequently alluded to in earlier anthropological writings. Largely using neurological models as metaphors, the references were very inexact. After Norbert Weiner worked out the principles of a feedback in his *Cybernetics* (1948) it became a fashionable word, but it was generally used in a partial sense to illustrate the counteractive influence of different tendencies upon each other, without defining the limits of the system nor explaining how the equivalent of an automatic control worked.[2] Evans-Pritchard worked out a systematic self-stabilizing interaction to account for otherwise inexplicable elements in the Nuer political system. There is no reason to think that his description of a feedback system in Nuer political life has further repercussions on contemporary thought. The idea may be treated as a minor contribution to systems analysis, though I reserve judgement against the possible day of its being more fully exploited.)

I propose to justify these claims to modernity by referring to Evans-Pritchard's own work programme, his lectures given at the Egyptian University in Cairo in the early 1930s. Here he grappled with these problems in the rough-hewn form they were then presented – as questions about the nature of primitive mentality. Now, of course, they come as questions about our own mentality. I will inevitably need to sketch in the state of the art as he had found it. Some biographical notes about his personality and fieldwork will be necessary to give an idea of the foundations of his originality.

2. Human Mental Faculties

In the 1920s, when Evans-Pritchard's training began, the central questions in anthropology related to the conditions of human knowledge. The context for comparing tribes with each other and with Europeans was the keen interest in the evolution of the cognitive faculties. There was no delimited specialism in a particular field. Anthropologists could offer ideas culled from anywhere – zoology, physics or primitive art. Everyone was interested in discovering psychological or physical or even social factors that influence perception. How sensations coming into the brain are received, organized and stored for retrieval by memory and how memory does its work were part of a general theorizing about perceptual processes that belonged to no one narrow province. Zoologists, psychologists, neurologists and other biological scientists could contribute, their results being taken into account by philosophers. Anthropologists could introduce into the discussions speculations based on the bizarre, extreme cases to which they had access. This was generally a healthy intervention, for scholars know that they are too prone to make their local experience represent the entire human race. However, one stroke in creating a division of labour leads to another. Even to this day the normal cognitive processes tend to be studied in the disciplines established in the heart of our culture, while irrational or deviant forms become the special field of the scholars who report them. So totemism, magic and taboo are assigned to anthropology, marking by their outlandish names the side-lines from which anthropologists make their contribution to understanding how the mind works.

The nineteenth-century imagination had been deeply impressed by the contrast between two of its favourite stereotypes, that of ancestral primitive man and that of modern, scientific man. Even now the fascination of the divide remains. Among scholars who collect and sift information on the human capacity for thought, many ignore the divide but deepen it by concentrating most of their energies upon the subject nearest home. This includes the majority of those working in the sociology of knowledge because, by its history and methods, sociology in general deals primarily with modern society. Then there are those thinkers whose attention is fixed precisely upon that divide. These are primarily the anthropologists. Among them some emphasize the boundary between primitive and modern ways of thought. They concentrate on elucidating words which are held to be characteristic of primitive thought, not of our own, such as taboo and totemism, which their approach treats as largely untranslatable emanations of other ways of life. Then there are anthropologists whose work seeks to lower that boundary which sets primitive thought as a thing apart from our own. Much of Evans-Pritchard's work was devoted to removing those misunderstandings about our own thought which made it plausible to distinguish it radically from the thought of spear-throwing, stonetool-using, bow-and-arrow technologists.

Nineteenth-century explorers tended to deliver extraordinary reports of the peoples they encountered. Though the hope of fame may have driven them through jungles and deserts hitherto unknown, many of them are doomed to be remembered only because of a fish or a plant named after them, or at best by a statue in a square. As an exception, Baron Von den Steinen, who explored the Amazon in the 1890s, would surely have been gratified to know that he provided material for a problem tough enough to exercise serious scholars for almost a hundred years. The problem arises from the thought-provoking way in which he reported the Bororo Indians of Central Brazil as declaring that they were red parakeets.[1] He saw at once that they could have possibly meant that they were like red parakeets, a metaphor, or that after death they would become red parakeets, a religious belief. He anticipated the distorting effects of translation and tried to phrase the pertinent questions to allow of no ambiguity. But ambiguity there was, and when his report was taken up in 1910 by the French philosopher Lucien Lévy-Bruhl, his refinements were lost.

Lévy-Bruhl treated the Bororo as a prime example of pre-logical thinking.

> 'The Bororo . . . boast that they are red araras (parakeets).' This does not merely signify that after their death they become araras, nor that araras are metamorphosed Bororos, and must be treated as such. It is something entirely different . . . It is not a name they give themselves, nor a relationship that they claim. What they desire to express by it is actual identity. That they can be both the human beings they are and the birds of scarlet plumage at the same time, Von den Steinen regards as inconceivable, but to the mentality that is governed by the law of participation there is no difficulty in the matter. All communities which are totemic in form admit of collective representations of this kind, implying similar identity of the individual members of a totemic group and their totem.[2]

For Lévy-Bruhl, the Bororo capacity to tolerate self-contradiction was another case of the totally different cognitive slant, the pre-logical characteristic, of primitive mentality. A number of thinkers down to the present day have made the Bororo declaration famous by quoting or trying to interpret it.[3] They are few compared with the anthropologists who have discussed totemism as a set of beliefs characteristic of peoples at a certain stage of evolution, or who have discussed similar beliefs in shared human identity with classes of animals to illustrate a general problem about cognitive differences between different cultures. Inevitably, in so much discussion, with so much evidence and relatively little sustained analysis, the contribution from the anthropologists' side-lines to the understanding of cognition has often been obfuscating. The general reader, faced by a vast and abstruse literature, may well suspect that some small detail is wrong with the explorers' reports or that something major is wrong with the theorizing. Figures of thought that would be unproblematic if located in the speech of politicians or (better still) in Aristotle or Shakespeare, become preposterously incompatible beliefs issuing from the minds of primitives, creating bizarre problems which nowadays only anthropologists take seriously.

Evans-Pritchard's entry into this discussion is that of the plain, commonsensical Englishman, trained in history, biased towards empiricism, and suspicious of grand theoretical schemes. He brought with him two commitments: one to the unitary character of human cognition, and one to the sociological analysis which would reveal it. The first commitment meant that he knew Lévy-Bruhl was mistaken, that to search for a distinctively primitive cognitive style was the wrong method for solving puzzles such as that posed by the Bororo: if we understood ourselves better, such puzzles could be treated as problems about our own styles of thought, so opening a shaft of light upon the human condition. The second commitment meant that he was determined to give a strong methodological edge to the speculations of the French sociologists in whose writings he saw the unrealized possibilities of a proper sociology of knowledge.

Robert Merton's review of the sociology of knowledge, which appeared in 1945,[4] distinguished an original German school starting from Marx and centring upon Marxist thought, a distinctively different French school whose work he suggested was 'largely autochthonous and independent of similar researches in Germany',[5] and later American developments. Though his omission of any British contribution is accurate, the connection between the French and German efforts was closer than his account recognized. The German dialogue, stemming as it did from Marxist historical materialism, was necessarily focused on the ideological division between classes. Marx had unequivocally stated a programme for the sociology of knowledge when he taught that even the definition of a problem depends on the experience of a particular historical way of living. German

Marxist discussion of sociology was radical and revolutionary. If at the turn of the century it crossed the border to France, it was understandable that it took a different focus. Moreover, France had already undergone the revolutionary blood-letting that served as a paradigm for all Europe. France had recently been invaded by Germany, and was to be so invaded twice again. The French ignored but were not ignorant of the German work. Their own approach was not so much independent but a larger response to the ideas from Germany, negating their value in the same spirit as the British psychologists denied the value of the French sociology of memory and perception. So it was that instead of being interested in class conflict, Durkheim was interested in group solidarity. His synthesis of then-current theories about the social construction of categories argued that shared categories of thought are a function of and a prerequisite for society. To teach this he turned away from European history and introduced accounts of very distant, very curious small societies.

Lévy-Bruhl's theory of primitive mentality owes very little to Durkheim. (He had actually written no less than eight books on philosophy before he turned to this topic.) He recognized that the so-called mystic participations of prelogical thought rested upon social institutions. But the occasional remarks he made about social conditions were never central to his thinking. He did not consider that his ideas needed to be developed by more research. He was satisfied to assert that primitive peoples had a different, mystical focus of attention, a different perception of relevant causal sequences, and a different logic.

Evans-Pritchard admired Lévy-Bruhl[6] and took his work as his own starting point in a programme addressed to every anthropologist who tried to explain magic in terms of weakness in the primitive mental equipment, susceptibility to strong emotions such as awe, anxiety or fear. The French sociologists used their notion of primitive psychology to support their position in an international and politically live argument about social solidarity, its sources and weaknesses.

Evans-Pritchard would use their leading ideas to sociologize theories of the mind that hitherto had no grounding in social theory.

In many respects the Anglo-Saxon anthropologists were unsophisticated and short of learning, and it is interesting to speculate whether the political neutrality which their work enjoyed was an impediment rather than a guarantee of intellectual freedom and power. To explain the peculiarities of primitive religion they made a naive appeal to psychology.

At Exeter College, R. R. Marett had taught a theory of the origin of religion, tracing it to a sense of awe, mystery and wonder, to which the primitive was supposed to be particularly alive.[7] In *The Golden Bough*, Frazer traced the religious history of mankind back to a contemplative, poetic sense, an emotional view of man and nature. Malinowski explained magic as response to anxiety;[8] others explained it by fear. Elliot Smith's argument, that all cultures can be traced back to their cradle in Egypt, like other ethnological schemes of the time, had to be supported by such an elaborate theory that it fell beneath the weight of its own implausible props.[9]

There is no need here to be more precise or more encyclopedic about the exotic ideas that were invented by Europeans to account for the newly discovered exotic beliefs of other peoples beyond the Judeo-Christian tradition. One gets the feeling that no theory would have been too peculiar to gain some acceptance : the one thing necessary for scholarly renown was to deal with a large enough body of evidence to be able to sweep the less amenable information under the carpet and force the small voice of common sense to mere piecemeal protests. One also gets the impression that the physical scientists who became anthropologists, perhaps for lack of a firm foothold in the discipline of their original training, failed to build up a solid institutional framework around their new calling. A sense of amateurishness hangs over the pronouncements of W. R. Rivers, H. C. Haddon, Perry and Elliot Smith. By contrast, the French sociologists of the same period succeeded in building up an institutional structure that provided internal canons of criticism and a steady development of ideas. The English were more like free-booters who raided when they felt like it, took only what they fancied, and furnished inaccessible hideouts with their scholarly loot. Nevertheless they all considered themselves to be contributing to knowledge about human cognition.

Take for example the career of A. C. Haddon whom Evans-Pritchard knew well.[10] Haddon had originally been trained as a zoologist at Cambridge. After an expedition to Melanesia to study marine biology, he published *The Decorative Art of New Guinea: a Study in Papuan Ethnography* (1894). I will not stress the fact that he plunged into art history with the most rudimentary preparation. In 1895 he wrote *Evolution in Art as Illustrated by the Life Histories* of Designs. Then in 1898–9 his career turned over full time to ethnology when he led a famous Cambridge expedition to the Torres Straits. The team he assembled were psychologists, linguists, musicians. Its work was from the beginning planned to contribute to the theory of memory and perception.

Haddon's book on *Evolution in Art* is concerned, as the title suggests, with how a design comes to life, as it were, flourishes and gets embellished, and then simplifies, loses its distinctive features, degenerates and dies. We can easily see now that the life-history approach has several difficulties. For one, it assumes that the scholar knows when the design is alive or dead; for another, he has already judged its degeneration by his own criteria of stability and simplification. The problem of artistic life, as Haddon put it, is that creativity is easily overwhelmed by inertia; we Europeans are abundantly energetic and creative, much less convention-ridden than the primitives, known to be dull and uninventive.

For Haddon, the big divide between primitives and moderns lay in the question: how do fruitful ideas come to an end? The answer to the problem in art would be the same as the answer for all civilization. Haddon invoked a theory of mental arrest copied on a physics model of loss of energy, which he developed from the ideas of Guillaume Ferrero, an Italian. Quoting Ferrero : 'By the law of mental inertia, the state of consciousness, image, idea, emotion – cannot last forever, after the exciting cause has ceased to exist – for a state of consciousness is a transformation of energy, and it finishes when it has exhausted its initial quantity.'[11] Haddon thought that the life-history of a design came to a halt when the image was fully standardized within a particular culture, or conventionalized. He focused attention on progressive loss of detail and loss of image, arranging his examples in a series from the richest to the simplest, showing how an alligator design or bird design could be transformed into a purely abstract scroll pattern. This process he called conventionalization.

The concept of conventionalization was immediately seized by Frederick Bartlett, the Cambridge experimental psychologist. Bartlett himself was well read in anthropology, and some of his friends were anthropologists famous in their day. He later said that in his twenties he had come closely under the influence of Dr Rivers, the anthropologist, and of Dr C. S. Myers, who was at that time the Head of the Department of Experimental Psychology at Cambridge.[12] (Both Rivers and Myers had been members of Haddon's expedition to the Torres Straits in 1898.) Haddon's work on conventionalization interested him because when studying

... perception sequences, it seemed there came a stage when something like a stored pattern or standard representation took charge of the observer's response and principally settled what he was alleged to have perceived. Moreover, observers of much the same social group were very likely to use the same stored standard representation.

Just about this time I had become interested in the ethnographical studies of the development of decorative art forms such, for example, as those undertaken by Dr A. C. Haddon in *The Decorative Art of New Guinea* (1894). It was from such writings that I borrowed the plan of attempting to derive and use sequences for perceiving and remembering so as to help towards an understanding of those processes of conventionalization which not only produce standards and patterns peculiar to the decorative art of a social group, but could also, it seemed to me, play an important part in the individual's interpretation of his own environment.

The programme was now moving away from straight-forward studies of the determining activities and conditions of perceiving and remembering, towards an all-out experimental attack on conventionalizing in both its individual and its social forms.[13]

Bartlett had earlier written *Psychology and Primitive Culture* (1923) in which he quoted many American and British anthropologists. His book started out with the assumption, established in philosophy and psychology, that the process of cognition is a selective screening and organizing of sensory inputs. But he was unusual in insisting that, the individual subject being always a social individual, the selective screening must be influenced by social experiences. He worked this out with many ethnographic examples. His analysis of the folk tale is particularly convincing: The search for the origins of a folk tale is futile; likewise the discovery of those grand archetypal themes dear to many psychologists, or the attempt to use folk tales to establish the history of past institutions. He said firmly,

It is not the institution that is derived from the story, but the story from the institution ... That the folk story is a social product implies, among other things, that in its matter the popular tale must make a common-sense appeal and in its form it must be shaped as to call forth a widely readily shared response. *For both of these characters spring from the fact that the folk story is largely a mode of social intercourse.*[14] [my italics]

Bartlett had important insights on taboo, which he in-

23

sisted was not to be explained by fear. Many writers of the time named fear as the primary emotion explaining taboos. 'But when we turn to popular stories ... descriptions of fear seem to occupy no very important position.'[15] Bartlett himself explained taboo by a sociological requirement to control conflict by separating spheres of action and even creating separate cognitive spheres. For 'the general determination of boundaries' and for the social control of curiosity, Bartlett's words were remarkably explicit: 'The history of any primitive group, in fact, reveals certain spheres of activity within which curiosity is not readily to be allowed full sway. The limitation does not necessarily produce disorder. Curiosity is assigned to its own realm.'[16]

This was a book to put into the hands of anthropologists, full of good sense and promise for a sociological approach to perception. In it, Bartlett had been fully committed to solving the problem of how social factors influence cognition. He knew and accepted that the problem of conventionalization could be solved only by knowing the institutions in which conventional responses were embedded. He had said so over and over again. However, when he went on later to write his justly famous book *Remembering* (1932), he had made very little progress towards a sociological theory of cognition.

Working on the psychology of memory, he planned to expand and test the idea of the neurologist Henry Head that each individual attends selectively to sensations whose stored results create a cumulatively developed schema. Head supposed the schema or armature of attention to be individual, but, as we have seen, Bartlett expected it to be institutionally anchored. But, he said of the attempted draft of a book about conventionalizing: 'There came a time when I began to write this book, and I laboured heavily through two or three chapters, but it did not go well. I tore up what I had written and for some time there followed a most unpleasant period when it seemed that I had taken a lot of steps to get nowhere at all.'

The young genius Norbert Weiner, who 'was at that time

in Cambridge studying mathematical logic', brought the barren period to an end by helpfully suggesting that 'the Russian Scandal' game be turned into an experimental method. An experimental subject was isolated and shown a picture; the picture then being taken away, the subject was asked to reproduce it. His drawing was then presented to the next subject who saw it equally briefly, lost it, and was asked to reproduce what he recalled, and so on until as many subjects as were required had worked on successive transformations of the original design. By this means he could show some of the perceptual processes that lead to a steady reproduction or to conventionalization.[17]

By two ideas, serial reproduction and subjective organization of experience, Bartlett had found a way of exploring memory and, through memory, recognition and other faculties of the mind. The work he then embarked on was immense. Each experiment that he counted successful led him to consider new ones. An inventor of methodologies and a supreme instrument-maker, he succeeded in showing how the perceiving subject organizes, constructs, maintains and defends the stability of its cognitive scheme. There was so much work to do in developing this approach that he relegated the programme of discovering the social foundation of stable perception. So he himself fulfilled his life-work's lesson. He had taught originally that social institutions accounted for memory and forgetting. The author of the best book on remembering forgot his own first convictions. He became absorbed into the institutional framework of Cambridge University psychology, and restricted by the conditions of the experimental laboratory.

Bartlett's work is relevant here because it establishes the claim that anthropology was expected to contribute to psychology in the 1920s and that close exchanges were made between those disciplines. It also illustrates the difficulty of creating a sociological theory of perception, and helps to explain why such a theory is still missing to this day.

Another reason for picking out Haddon and Bartlett to illustrate this earlier period, rather than Rivers, Radcliffe-

Brown or Malinowski is the evidence showing that Evans-Pritchard adopted Bartlett's research interests and even used the same vocabulary about selective principles of attention for indicating what he held to be the central problems. He is also the only anthropologist in England whose work provides this continuous relationship with a major concern in perception psychology.

In the 1920s the most popular models for the processes of human reasoning were borrowed from the physical sciences, and the best were neurological. In addition to Henry Head, Sherrington was enormously influential for anthropology. He worked out the neural connections in the spinal column and brain stem that sustain the normal maintenance of muscle-tone and of posture and reflex movements in the limbs. Then, moving on from the spinal column and brain stem to the fore-brain of the cat and ape, he mapped the motor keyboard of the cerebral cortex.

So many of Sherrington's concepts were borrowed, extended, transformed by thinkers in other fields that it is impossible to separate threads in what became a common canopy of ideas. Take his demonstration of reciprocal innervation, the principle by which antagonistic muscles must relax to allow the contraction of the muscles that cause a limb to move. In sociology, Bartlett tried to focus on 'group difference' tendencies that clustered about various forms of institutions, and insisted that it is not enough to know what these tendencies are; one must also study the relationship they bear to one another; particularly, he was interested in the 'conflict of tendencies and their mutual reinforcement',[18] and in processes of inhibiting antagonism. This sounds so like a vague version of Freud's model of the mind, as well as Sherrington's neurological model, that it is clear that the basic idea of reciprocal interplay between forces was freely available to contemporary thought.

An important disseminator of Sherrington's ideas in the 1920s was Eugenio Rignano (1870–1930). An Italian professor of philosophy who wrote on many topics and was quickly translated in French and English, Rignano worked out what he called a mnemonic explanation of attention. He had a systematic theory of mental functions: the whole organism was always involved, he argued, and for a human being the concept of the whole organism would have to include its social ambience. He took over Sherrington's distinction between non-distance perceptors (which 'permit immediate or almost immediate satisfaction of the affective tendencies with which they start') and distance perceptors (which can hold the state of attention in suspense). Among his examples: the sea anemone does not pay attention or react to the presence of food except when its metabolism has reached a state requiring more nutrient. In man, the experience of hunger, a particular localized sensation in the wall of the stomach, is enough to cause the same acts that would be induced by real hunger. Long before starvation is threatened, the immediate perception of hunger has reminded the human organism that it needs nourishment; long before death from thirst, a local sensation in the mouth and throat is a warning request for attention; the species will die out if not reproduced, but the sexual urge is called into action without waiting for the species' survival to be at risk. Rignano said that in these forms we find the substitution of the part for the whole: thirst and sexual hunger are examples of the mnemonic process by which the needs of the whole organism are continually met by short-lived local transfers of attention – early-warning reminders, as it were.

The array of slow and quick nerve pathways to the brain, the concept of reciprocal innervation, the power to suspend attention – these three ideas appear later in Evans-Pritchard's work. At least his debt here can be tracked, for several times he acknowledged Rignano's book *The Psychology of Reasoning*. He even placed Rignano alongside William James in his programmatic statement about the need to understand the selective principles controlling attention. On this issue, the difference between Evans-Pritchard and anyone else in England (apart from Bartlett) was his confidence that the selective principles were to be found in social institutions, and that fieldwork was the way to find them. Seen in this light, his life can be presented as a tribute to the French sociologists, Durkheim, Mauss,[19] Lévy-Bruhl and Halbwachs,[20] potential collaborators who worked on the same problems of perception but were rejected by psychologists on the English side of the Channel.[21] The failure of British psychologists to develop a sociological dimension to their experimental thinking, and the failure of the French to benefit from the British methodological advances, are themselves problems for the sociology of knowledge that are not explained by their not knowing of each other's work. They read, but they misunderstood.

3. The Continuity of Evans-Pritchard's Programme

This statement, made in 1934, may be taken as a summary of the theoretical interests and the field in which Evans-Pritchard intended to work:

> As James, Rignano, and others, have shown, any sound or sight may reach the brain of a person without entering into his consciousness. We may say that he 'hears' or 'sees' it but does not 'notice' it. In a stream of sense impressions only a few become conscious impressions and these are selected on account of their greater affectivity. A man's interests are the selective agents and these are to a great extent socially determined for it is generally the value attached to an object by all members of a social group that directs the attention of an individual towards it.
>
> It is, therefore, a mistake to say that savages perceive mystically or that their perception is mystical. On the other hand we may say that savages pay attention to phenomena on account of the mystical properties with which their society has endowed them, and that often their interest in phenomena is mainly, even exclusively, due to these mystic properties.[1]

The statement points to society as the whole field of human interests and thus as the source of the selective principle which controls attention.

In planning this book, I checked Evans-Pritchard's footnotes and bibliographic references, trying to work out his intellectual origins. In his later writing, punctiliousness in gratefully acknowledging every missionary's or district officer's evidence on every conceivable fieldwork topic seemed to be paralleled by virtual silence as to his intellectual debts. The relation of his ethnographic researches to contemporary speculations or theory was never spelled out in his big fieldwork monographs. As a matter of principle these were written with practically no polemics, no controversies, no disputatious threshing out of definitions. Evans-Pritchard did not think it right to use the ethnographic reporting for a forum for personal triumphs against rival theories. The task of ethnographic presentation was too solemn and too difficult. The anthropologist had to use his scholarly and sociological sense to present a coherent story, omitting nothing, twisting nothing and adding nothing that could not be justified. The theoretical burden would be found in the internal consistency of a large body of ethnographic analysis, in which other ethnographers would discern theoretical innovation. In his big books on the Nuer, the Azande and the Bedouin there is little guidance to the layman as to what they were meant to contribute to twentieth-century controversy. Later, general statements, in pamphlets and papers written after his fieldwork days were over, were written for students and the general public; their style is bland, as if everything were terribly obvious. But reflection on his whole opus made me realize that the life plan of intellectual effort had already been mapped out very clearly in the three essays published in the *Bulletin of the Faculty of Arts* of the Egyptian University : 'The Intellectualist (English) Interpretation of Magic' (1933); 'Lévy-Bruhl's Theory of Primitive Mentality' (1934) and 'Science and Sentiment : An Exposition and Criticism of the Writings of Pareto' (1936). These essays are mature, considered statements of the programme on which Evans-Pritchard was already well-embarked. The students of the faculty of arts of Fouad I University had been privileged to hear their teacher's long-term agenda of publications explained and justified. Here we get plenty of controversy, denunciations, sarcasm, hard-hitting argumentation. On the evidence of these essays, Evans-Pritchard fully intended his work as a major contribution to a sociological theory of knowledge.

The first essay was on the subject of magic. It would be easier and more in the mood of this exercise to use the word 'foreign' where 'primitive' or 'savage' ways of thought are referred to. But it would be worse than a mere anachronism to do so. The charge of weak logic or impaired reasoning faculties gained all its interest precisely because it was not laid to the door of all foreigners but applied to people called primitive and therefore in some sense like our forebears. The notion that their minds were still in thrall to magic romanticized the subject, while it justified its seriousness by suggesting evolutionary trends to which all human society was supposedly subject. It will be necessary to use the terms 'primitive thought' and 'primitive magic', though Evans-Pritchard's own work should by now have dismantled the difference.

'Magic' was the one word that focused the discussion in his day. Primitives believed in magic, and we did not. Magic contrasted with the style of thought in a modern Western-type society, technologically superior, with its knowledge of the external world soundly based on scientific principles. But it was important, said Evans-Pritchard, to clarify the point that scientific thought is a very specialized experience that only takes place in very specialized conditions. Those who engage in it do not engage in it all the time : when they are out of the laboratory they think like everyone else does every day. The contrast between primitives and ourselves is much exaggerated by pretending that we think scientifically all the time. To prevent that error the proper method is to compare like with like, our everyday thought with their everyday thought. Immediately the investigation is shifted to a lower level. Everyday language and everyday thought set into their situational context have to be the subject of enquiry. Not only do we not conduct our lives as if we were conducting scientific experiments, but we do not think about the subject-matter of religion as if we were theologians. The anthropological discussion had become hopelessly obfuscated by false and arbitrary abstractions. Particularly, the cogitations of the primitive upon his luck, his hopes, his death and judgement (no more jumbled, nor less, than our own upon the same subjects) had been erected into a complex structure of thought. Worthy of the name philosophy only by virtue of its complexities, a total fabrication of the investigator, primitive thought was never a philosophy subscribed to by any one at any time, but the result of weary replies to relentless interrogators who knew from their own religious background what questions to ask and what answers to count or discount. So a crazy patchwork theorizing, spun from the mind of the enquirer, was doing duty for the primitive in contrast with an equally unrealistic representation of modern thought.

For example, Evans-Pritchard said: Lévy-Bruhl

was not really comparing what savages think with what Europeans think but the systematized ideology of savage cultures with the content of individual minds in Europe. His authorities had collected all the information they could get about the mystical beliefs held by a community of savages about some phenomenon and pieced them together into a coordinated ideological structure. These beliefs, like the myths which Europeans also record, may have been collected over a long period of time and from dozens of informants. The resulting pattern of belief may be a fiction since it may never be actually present in a man's consciousness at any time and may not even be known to him in its entirety. This fact would have emerged if records of everything a savage does and says throughout a single day were recorded for then we would be able to compare our own thoughts more adequately with the real thoughts of savages instead of with an abstraction pieced together from persistent enquiries conducted in an atmosphere quite unlike that of the savage's ordinary milieu and in which it is the European who evokes the beliefs by his questions rather than the objects with which they are associated ... Moreover, primitive thought as pieced together in this manner by European observers is full of contradictions which do not arise in real life because the bits of belief are evoked in different situations.[2]

He makes the same complaint against Pareto :

> He intends to study the part played by logical, and the part played by non-logical, thought and behaviour side by side, and in interaction, in the same culture. His intention was excellent. In fact, however, he does not adhere to this plan. He writes at great length about fallacious beliefs and irrational behaviour but he tells us very little about common-sense beliefs and empirical behaviour ... If Pareto for civilized peoples, and Lévy-Bruhl for savages, had given us a detailed account of their real life during an ordinary day we would be able to judge whether their non-logical behaviour is as qualitatively and quantitatively important as the writers' selective methods would lead us to suppose. Actually, I would contend, non-logical conduct plays a relatively minor part in the behaviour of either primitive or civilized men and is relatively of minor importance.[3]

Note Evans-Pritchard's demand for an account of real life in an ordinary day and the rejection of misleading distinctions between primitives and moderns.

> Pareto's work is an amusing commentary on Lévy-Bruhl's books. Lévy-Bruhl has written several volumes to prove that savages are pre-logical in contrast to Europeans who are logical. Pareto has written several volumes to prove that Europeans are non-logical. It would therefore seem that no one is mainly controlled by reason anywhere or at any epoch.[4]

Here in embryo is Evans-Pritchard's critique of the concepts of reason and rationality as the philosophers use the terms. 'Indeed one of the reasons why I have chosen to analyse Pareto's treatise is to bring out the fact that a study of unscientific thought and ritual behaviour cannot be restricted to primitive societies but must be extended to civilized societies also.'[5] Evans-Pritchard's method requires com-

E-P.—B

mon sense to be compared with common sense, ritual with ritual, theology with theology, so that the appropriate level may be kept. In its full development the method requires the context of belief and behaviour to be specified. Demanding the social context for interpreting utterances was Malinowski's great teaching.[6] But Evans-Pritchard was to go much further in defining social contexts. At this early stage, he explicitly praised Lévy-Bruhl for perceiving that the publicly known clusters of ideas which he called collective representations 'are functions of institutions, so that we may suppose as social structures vary, the collective representations will show concomitant variations.'[7] But Lévy-Bruhl did not follow up the implications of this remarkable quotation. In fact, Evans-Pritchard seems to have set him up as a straw man, for Lévy-Bruhl had surely not realized the significance of the sociological remarks he occasionally threw in or he could not have written so much about prelogical mentality. Evans-Pritchard makes these failings quite clear.

> Whom is one to accuse of 'prelogical mentality', the South African missionaries or the Negroes of whom they record that 'they only believe what they see' and that 'in the midst of the laughter and applause of the populace, the heathen enquirer is heard saying 'Can the God of the white men be seen with our eyes?' ... Both missionaries and Negroes alike were dominated by the collective representations of their cultures. Both were alike critical when their thought was not determined by social doctrines.[8]

In these three early lectures, Evans-Pritchard dismissed the terms 'illogical', 'non-logical' and 'pre-logical' from the discussion of primitive mentality. Scientific thought was not to be recognized merely by living with its results in a technologically advanced society. At this stage he followed Pareto's division of thought into two categories, the logico-experimental and the non-logico-experimental : the former is scientific and the latter is not. But it was still necessary to insist that thought that is coherently built up from valid inferences is not necessarily defective in logic; with irreproachable logic it can be very defective in its description of reality from the point of view of any foreign culture. If the premises are different, equally correct reasoning will lead to a different picture of the world.

At this stage of the argument, Evans-Pritchard felt he needed a definition of scientific notions; he derived it from his own cultural tradition : [9] Standing square to the ontology of his own culture, he felt able to use the word 'mystical' for beliefs in entities and powers which did not enter into the logico-experimental account of objective reality. He stayed with that word to the last, finding it useful, even though he had long since discarded the word 'supernatural'.[10] But when he uses 'mystical' there is no hint of derogatory judgement. Those experiences which the scientific culture cannot include within objective reality are labelled mystical, but not judged either real or unreal. He made a great point of taking their reality as seriously as do the people who create and live with mystic powers and entities.

We would surely not wish our idea about the nature of reality to be frozen at any one particular moment in the development of science. Might it not have been wiser for Evans-Pritchard to have kept silent altogether about objective reality? Some philosophical commentators have used his work to support their denial that systematic comparison between cultures is possible. This is just as contrary to his thought as it is mistaken to use his work for imagining cultures based on alternative logic or on non-logical thinking. Evans-Pritchard believed in making comparison possible and expected it to be possible by studying different responses to misfortune. His method of research implicitly anchored each local version of reality to the local system of accountability.

It is good to pause here to observe how his own independent reasoning brought him to two principles enunciated in Wittgenstein's *Philosophical Investigations* and much cited as clues to the latter's work. Both thinkers were forced to struggle out of the toils of existing speculative formulations, and both saw that the meanings of thoughts and words had to be located in social activity.

Evans-Pritchard was in the middle of fieldwork when he delivered his lectures in Egypt, but he had not yet written the first of his books. In the lectures he straightened out the current entanglements. The programme he wrote for himself would abhor speculative abstractions. There would be evidence for everything he reported. The facts would not be selected by subjective bias. They would not be selected from hundreds of societies. The evidence would not be hearsay; it would not be elicited by interrogation; it would not be purely verbal. Assuming that words and ideas are inextricable from the rest of social action, an interpretation would be upheld by complete description of the rules governing the action in which the speech occurs.

Looking back at his work as a whole and trying to trace the main influences on him, it seems extraordinary that he did not know what Wittgenstein was saying, or how closely they parallelled each other. But apparently the convergence results not from contact but from similar historical pressures. Once the trail is laid, anyone who reads the *Philosophical Investigations* will see even richer convergences, and further implications from Evans-Pritchard's scrupulous working out of a method and its philosophy.

First, take Wittgenstein's insistence that the speaking of a language is part of activity and that it only makes sense when the rest of the activity is known: '... the term "language-game" is meant to bring into prominence that the speaking of a language is part of an activity, or of a form of life.' 'Think of the tools in a box ...'. Searching for a meaning is 'like looking into a cabin of a locomotive'. It is 'easy to think of a language consisting only of orders and reports in battle'.[11] Then there is the distinction to be made between the core of fundamental assumptions (the total system of hypotheses) and, on the other hand, the inductive reasoning that it makes possible. Deep assumptions about the universe that arise from how people live together are unchallengeable and largely un-inspectable. Somewhere reasoning has to come to an end; it stops at these assumptions. Why are the people so certain that they are right and the missionary's story is wrong? Because they have to live and act: action proceeds upon decisions and decisions upon assumptions, but the assumptions anticipate possibilities of action. 'Whether the earlier experience is the cause of the certainty depends on the system of hypotheses, of natural laws, in which we are considering the phenomenon of certainty. Is our confidence justified? – What people accept as justification – is shown by how they think and live.' 'We expect this, and are surprised *at that*. But the chain of reasoning has an end.'[12] That it has to have an end is reasonable enough; but how it comes to an end and what that end is like, how it can be recognized, is not foreseen in the *Philosophical Investigations* or in the many commentaries upon it. Evans-Pritchard's method of tracing meanings through the process of fixing human accountability uncovers the fundamental system of hypotheses, both where the chain of reasoning stops and where its links are forged.

Many anthropologists, even recently, have adopted the theory of knowledge that Wittgenstein attributed to St Augustine, one in which words are assumed to correlate with, or stand for, particular meanings. The result is a triad containing reality, a set of concepts about reality, and a system of signs which signify the concepts: meaning is turned into a limited item, or at least a limited set of possible transformations, and much philosophical enquiry has focused upon the relation between the case as it is and the case that is given in the concepts. Wittgenstein tried to shift the focus of enquiry from an abstracted set of concepts, chosen and groomed to be worked upon by philosophers, towards the idea of meanings generated in active exchanges within the framework of human intentions. The value of knowledge is to be found not in its firm anchorage in some postulated fixed reality, but in its service within the rules devised for achieving some human ends. The entanglements of philosophy come from false abstractions, taking thoughts out of context and giving thought to thoughts about thoughts: 'Like an engine idling, not when it is doing work.'[13] This exactly parallels Evans-Pritchard on the over-formalization and false abstractions of Frazer and Lévy-Bruhl. Of clarifications in philosophy, Wittgenstein said: 'What we are destroying is nothing but houses of cards, and we are clearing up the ground of language on which they stand. The results of philosophy are the uncovering of one or another piece of plain nonsense and bumps that the understanding has got by running its head up against the limits of language.'[14]

If we follow closely Evans-Pritchard's methods along this same path, we will find some of Wittgenstein's enigmas clarified. Anthropology can add something to the idea of the limits of knowledge, or the 'limits of the world', a re-iterated phrase in Wittgenstein. Evans-Pritchard has a method to contribute to the idea of perspicuous representation (or the transparent proof and overview which carries conviction); he has something to say about the grounds or conditions that make knowledge possible; and something positive to say about the possibilities of comparison between societies that has been doubted by Wittgenstein's followers. At these points Evans-Pritchard's work entered a conversation for which it was ready but in whose cogs it has not even yet been fully engaged. He started by seeking the selective principles governing attention, and started (thanks to the French colleagues) by expecting the principles to lie in social interaction. He had to cut through the methodological entanglements we have described; this greatly increased his sensitivity to the question of what can be taken as evidence. In his dealing with that question he opened the other doors one by one.

4. Fieldwork Methods

It would be easy for an English anthropologist, coming after Malinowski and taking the perspectives of the French sociologists of *L'Année Sociologique* seriously, to see that the next step would have to be the systematic gathering of information by rigorously controlled methods. Evans-Pritchard's Egyptian essays show clearly how defective were the sources currently being used in all anthropological controversies.

In the history of anthropology, new stages in the development of fieldwork provide just as distinctive markers of new periods as the development of telescopes in astronomy. Before the turn of the century the main sources of information for anthropology were the detailed monographs of missionaries who had spent their lives among the people whose customs they wrote about. The anthropologists who pondered upon these materials came from literary, classical and legal studies. They corresponded with the travellers, merchants, administrators and missionaries, and interpreted their reports according to the current theories. No one thought of doing systematic fieldwork. Indeed a naive belief persisted that the facts collected and combined in this way into theories were somehow pure facts, unbiased by theory-making. The two processes, collecting facts and theorizing, were held to be as different as spinning and weaving, with a more resounding glory to be earned by the weaver of theories.[1] Heaven forbid! Sir James Frazer had replied to William James's enquiry about natives he might have known himself.[2]

Eventually library analysis gave way to the next stage when physical scientists replaced the literary philosophers in anthropology. Boas,[3] a physicist and geographer, led expeditions to Baffin Island and British Columbia. A. C. Haddon, as we have seen, originally a marine biologist, led an expedition to Melanesia in 1898. With him went experts in psychology, medicine, linguistics and music. C. G. Seligman was one of those who accompanied Haddon to Melanesia; he later organized surveys of African cultures on which he employed Evans-Pritchard as research assistant.[4]

The next development, after the grand surveys and expeditions, led to the full professionalization of anthropology as a career. This was inaugurated by Malinowski, who is recognized as the father of modern anthropology because of his high standards for fieldwork.[5] Evans-Pritchard, however, insisted that Malinowski share the credit with A. R. Radcliffe Brown, saying that the latter, being much the abler thinker, had been the first to do intensive fieldwork with a sociological framework of ideas and had described the social life of the Andaman Islanders with some kind of theoretical position to develop. Malinowski had indubitably spent much longer in one study of a single people, the Tobriand Islanders of Melanesia. He spent four whole years – during the 1914–18 war – in their midst. He was the first anthropologist to conduct his research through the native language and the first to live in the centre of the life he was recording: 'In these favorable circumstances Malinowski came to know the Tobriand Islanders well, and he was describing their social life in a number of bulky and some shorter monographs up to the time of his death.'[6] This half-hearted praise implied it was a piece of luck to get the credit for developing a new method just because of an enforced stay of four years among delightful palm trees and lagoons, with barely two theoretical notions to rub together, no formulated problems, no sharp cutting edge for any investigation and no controlled comparisons.

Between Radcliffe Brown's greater theoretical strength and his weaknesses in fieldwork, and Malinowski's theoretical softness and field strength, Evans-Pritchard, writing this comparison, could have felt his own record of African fieldwork made a fair bid to have surpassed them both at their best. His study of the Azande was based on twenty months of fieldwork. His research among the Nuer totalled only one year. But each expedition was organized so systematically that one aspect of life analysed in detail contributed to understanding another and another until a consistent picture emerged in the round. He studied and wrote briefly upon other peoples of the Sudan. In the Second World War, as political officer to the British Administration of Cyrenaica, in Libya, he collected the historical and ethnographic information for a book on the Sanusiya, an Islamic religious order. Others have spent longer in fieldwork, spread their energies over more areas, or concentrated more single-mindedly upon one small place. But none, I think, has so systematically organized the ethnography of a cultural region and brought to three intensive studies such a sustained enquiry.

Trained by C. G. Seligman, Evans-Pritchard first conducted ethnological surveys in the Sudan. This meant tracing the territorial spread of a people, mapping the boundaries of their language and culture, and the boundaries of their political domain. Such a survey was normally carried out very quickly, with visits lasting from one day to a few weeks at the outside, using questioning, working through interpreters and selected informants. After he had helped to collect information for Seligman's *Survey of the Pagan Tribes of the Nilotic Sudan*, Evans-Pritchard started real fieldwork. According to his own teaching, the anthropologist

must live as far as possible in their villages and camps, where he is, again as far as possible, physically and morally part of the community ... This is not merely a matter of physical proximity. There is also a psychological side to it. By living among the natives as far as he can like one of themselves the anthropologist puts himself on a level with them. Unlike the administrator and missionary he has no authority and status to maintain, and unlike them he has a neutral position. He is not there to change their way of life but as a humble learner of it; and he has no retainers and intermediaries who obtrude between him and the people, no police, interpreters, or catechists to screen him off from them.[7]

Colonel Larken, the District Commissioner, has described how Evans-Pritchard worked:

> He immediately plunged straight into Zande life, though speaking no Zande, and having, as his servants, boys that spoke no other language. It was his idea that this drastic method would force him to pick up the language more quickly than any other, and that while he was doing so he would be able to absorb the local atmosphere. He had his house built in one of Chief Gangura's villages, and lived a most uncomfortable life, doing it deliberately to get close to the people he wished to observe. He was remarkably quick in learning enough Zande to start his interrogations, which he pursued with intense and most conscientious care ... His sympathetic approach and friendliness endeared him to all, and his manner was an ideal one for persuading them to tell him anything he wished to know.
>
> With his knowledge for a guide, one can now form a just appreciation of Zande actions and reactions which might otherwise appear incomprehensible or even blameworthy. No doubt many people will, thanks to him, escape unjust punishments, and receive a favourable response to their often obscure requests.[8]

From Evans-Pritchard's writing it is easy to guess now what these obscure requests were about. The everyday thought of the Azande was dominated by a theory of misfortune caused by witchcraft, and their other anxieties were all ultimately translatable into a concern to work the oracles that would warn them of witchcraft and to obtain the magic to fend it off or punish it.

Carrying out his precepts to the letter, Evans-Pritchard even conducted his own life by following the advice of oracles. He said that he took care 'to enact the same procedure as Azande and to take oracular verdicts as they take them. I always kept a supply of poison for the use of my household and we regulated our affairs in accordance with the oracle's decision. I may say that I found it as satisfactory a way of running my home and affairs as any other I know of.'[9]

He had chosen the Azande for his first major fieldwork because he was attracted by their friendly sophistication. His next fieldwork was no choice of his. An urgent request from the government of the Sudan called him to report on an unruly Nilotic tribe whose insurrection would be put down by force unless someone could interpret their intentions. He says that he agreed only after hesitation and misgivings: 'I was anxious to complete my study of the Azande before embarking on a new task. I also knew that a study of the Nuer would be extremely difficult. Their country and character are alike intractable and what little I had previously seen of them convinced me that I would fail to establish friendly relations with them.'[10]

However, Evans-Pritchard felt he had a responsibility as an anthropologist, because there was the risk that unless some trusted means of communication could be established, the Nuer would fight until they were destroyed. His assessment of the difficulties was completely right. But it now seems that nothing had happened to him before, that he had hardly started to discover his own humanity and the height of his powers until he lived among the Nuer. This is the dedication to his first book on them:

> Ah, the land of the rustling of wings, which is beyond the rivers of Ethiopia: that sendeth ambassadors by the sea, even in vessels of papyrus upon the waters, (saying) Go ye swift messengers, to a nation tall and smooth, to a people terrible from their beginning onward; a nation that meteth out and treadeth down, whose land the rivers divide. (Isaiah xviii: 1–2)

When he had completed his last volume on the Nuer, he seems to lay down the pen with a sigh of fulfilment: 'It is sad that I must now say a final farewell to a people who have for so many years occupied my thoughts. I was ... an alien sojourner, among them for only a year, but it was a year's relation of great intensity, and the quality of a relationship counts far more than its duration. This final volume of my trilogy is dedicated to them in memory of an experience which has greatly influenced my life.'[11]

Even the short account I shall give of the theoretical insights he gained through working with them will be suggestive of what they meant for him. The Nuer forced him to carry out his own precepts : to be respectful of the people he was studying; to be humble before them, an equal and no more; to depend on them. The twelve months' total of fieldwork was scraped together, seven weeks here, three months there, another month somewhere else and then back again : it was continually hindered or interrupted by illness, by political difficulties ('A government force surrounded our camp one morning at sunrise, searched for two prophets who had been leaders in a recent revolt'), by drought, by diplomatic delays.

In their way of initiating him to their life Nuer were like Zen masters, mocking and cruel, childish and clever at once. Eventually he and they crossed the dividing distance between them :

> As I became more friendly with the Nuer and more at home in their language they visited me from early morning till late at night, and hardly a moment of the day passed without men, women, or boys in my tent ... These endless visits entailed constant badinage and interruption and, although they offered opportunity for improving my knowledge of the Nuer language, imposed a severe strain. Nevertheless, if one chooses to reside in a Nuer camp one must submit to Nuer custom, and they are persistent and tireless visitors. The chief privation was the publicity to which all my actions were exposed, and it was long before I became hardened, though never entirely insensitive, to performing the most intimate operations before an

audience or in full view of the camp ... Azande would not allow me to live as one of themselves; Nuer would not allow me to live otherwise. Among Azande I was compelled to live outside the community; among Nuer I was compelled to be a member of it. Azande treated me as a superior; Nuer as an equal.[12]

Among the Azande he interrogated, among the Nuer he could only gather information in particles, not 'in chunks supplied by selected and trained informants'. No sneaking British love for amateurism has slipped in here. The new professionalism in fieldwork was not to rely on trained informants – it was to use participant observation first and formulate questions afterwards in the light of field experiences. But this is not to say that the new fieldwork was unsystematic. On the contrary the village census, the genealogy, the biography became established methods of checking and validating what might otherwise seem to be subjective impressions.[13]

The Nuer experience preceded Evans-Pritchard's close encounter with Islam provided by war-time service. The trail of his fieldwork itself is a guide to his own development. From the crafty, charming Azande, who considered every neighbour to be a potential witch and calmly took magic measures to combat witchcraft dangers, he learned to expand his West European view of rationality to include worlds built upon other assumptions than we subscribe to. Going from the Azande to the Nuer he had to reformulate the careful boundaries he had earlier drawn between mystic and rational, everyday reason and scientific thinking. Naked and simple, the Nuer opened vistas of other constructed universes, richer, nobler and better substantiated than any in Europe's romantic visions of the savage. After the Nuer he was ready to encounter Islam. In 1944 he entered the Roman Catholic Church. Some have regarded this step as a change of direction, but he insisted that it was no sudden break with his past but the latest step in a steady development of one who had always been a Catholic at heart.[14]

An historian might say that some anthropologist was bound to feel the pressure to combine the traditions of French speculative theorizing and English fieldworking empiricism. This would be a deterministic approach to the history of ideas. Evans-Pritchard's own approach to sociology was anti-deterministic, focused on men's purposes and their choices in dealing with one another. Indeed his career was very much the product of personal choices, not of impersonal convergent forces. This is the place to enter a comment on the personality of the anthropologist. He chose to combine the work of a scholar conversant with many languages with the life of a man of action, travelled in many lands.[15] He praised desert landscapes, loved Persian poetry and could recite reams of it by heart in English translation. He himself translated Arabic hymns and elegies into a style of English verse that confirmed the remark that his taste in poetry was Victorian and romantic.[16] His gift for friendship was enriched by extraordinary intuition and sensitivity.

A good insight into his attitudes comes from reading his *The Sanusi of Cyrenaica* (1949). The interruption of research imposed by war-time military service in Syria and Libya had renewed the contact with Bedouin Arabs begun with his teaching in Egypt ten years before. He evidently rejoiced in the chance to be immersed in Arabic civilization. Before writing the next outstanding book on the Nuer he paid a debt to Islam. Better than anything else he wrote, his history of the Sanusi order in Cyrenaica explains his recurrent shafts of criticism against reductionist theorizing and against sociological determinism. By a tour de force his combination of anthropology and history paid tribute to great personalities, so making explicit the voluntarist principles of his private philosophy. His sympathy for guerrilla herdsmen, their courage and conviction, illumines his own academic vendettas. A venomous wit made enemies of those with whom his disagreement went to a deep personal level where loyalty and integrity were at issue.

The Sanusiya is an Islamic Brotherhood, an order of Sufis

or Darwishes. Of Sufi mysticism, Evans-Pritchard wrote that it fills the need of simple people for warmth and colour in religion and provides personal contact and tenderness in the cult of saints.

> In every religion there will be found people who, like the Sufis, feel that while final acceptance of the tenets of the faith and conscientious performance of its duties are sufficient for righteousness and salvation, they do not satisfy the deeper longings of the soul which seeks always by entire love of God a perfect communion with Him. Human souls are rays of the divine sun imprisoned in the material world of the senses. The aim of Sufism has been to transcend the senses and to attain through love identification with God so complete that there is no longer a duality of 'God' and 'I', but there is only 'God'.[17]

Asceticism, isolation, contemplation, charity and religious exercises producing a state of ecstasy characterized the Sufi way of life. However, the Bedouin of Cyrenaica, among whom the Sanusiya Brotherhood was established in 1843, were not given to demonstrative, still less ecstatic forms of worship. It was 'difficult to imagine them piercing their cheeks with skewers, eating glass or swaying into convulsions'. Moreover, they had only the slightest knowledge of the Sanusi teachings or ritual. Evans-Pritchard addressed his book to explaining the historic association between these thoroughly pragmatic people and their learned and spiritual leaders.

The answer partly lies in the lineage structure of Bedouin internal rivalries. The Bedouin welcomed independent arbitration, and the immigrant tribes and their saintly lineages were glad to provide it (an anthropological approach). The rest of the answer lies in the pressures of Italian colonialism and war (a historical approach). The personalities of Sanusi leaders fused with the fiery independence and physical endurance of Bedouin herdsmen. Evans-Pritchard's book, which has been deeply influential among students of Arab civilization, can be seen as his second manifesto or guideline. It affirms the power of personal interventions in historical events. In this respect it carries the spirit of his postwar writing as clearly as the Egyptian lectures had outlined his early programme of research.

5. Accountability among the Azande

The anthropologist is forced by fieldwork to treat words as part of actions simply because in situations being observed the words so often have a definite performative role. Austin[1] mentions the placing of bets and the naming of ships as examples of words which, once spoken, permanently alter a situation. Writing similarly of words, Aaron Cicourel insists that all speech, not just the ritually distinctive forms, has a constitutive function.[2] The policeman's warning: 'Anything you say now may be taken down and used as evidence against you,' no more than the host's form of greeting and farewell, and the guest's murmurs of appreciation, constitutes an event as one of a particular kind. Because of the words, the things that have happened are classed in certain ways, entailing certain consequences that would not have followed if the various speeches had not been uttered. If this is true at all times, how much more striking are the declaratory, performative and constitutive aspects of speech when the words are magic spells. There we go – immediately plunged into the problem of defining magic. But Evans-Pritchard obviated it by recognizing one world of existences (that assumed by logico-experimental scientific thought of his own day) and being prepared to find other worlds with different beings and powers, justified by other assumptions locked into other institutional commitments. By declaring his own epistemological stand he could observe the other games.

The Azande put their most anxious problems to the poison oracle. Consulting the oracle, Evans-Pritchard tells us, involves feeding the poison to a chicken and addressing it clearly in words. The poison is told to kill the chicken if the answer is 'Yes'; the second time round for the same question it is told to kill the chicken if the answer is 'No'. Evidently the poison can understand, it acts intelligently, but

49

it must obey; it has no discretion to reveal or hide the truth, no will; it is not a person or any kind of spiritual being, only a delicate piece of technology. The oracle is vulnerable to certain contaminations, but unerring in its answers if properly protected and approached. There is no little person hidden inside the poison; the Azande deride the idea that just because it can answer questions it might be a person, as an example of British simplicity. But all oracles by their function have to be able to understand. That this one is addressed in words does not raise more of a problem about Azande credulity than an oracle addressed with twigs or bones or tea leaves. Precise speech is necessary in this case because the consulter wants to know who is bewitching his affairs. To put the names correctly, in order of plausibility as potentially malevolent persons, is a necessary part of the action. But the speech, however precise, is only a small part of the consultation. To get the full meaning, the anthropologist has to track all the pathways of possible action against a rival or unfriendly neighbour. In the end (and there tends to be an end) the oracle enables someone to be held accountable. The evidence for the anthropologist includes what the Azande say and also what they do. They hold each other accountable and their tracing of accountability does not stop even after the arbitration of death.

The question of magic has decisively shifted : the anthropologist is not wondering whether to classify the people as animistic or pre-animistic, magical or religious. The matter of slotting their beliefs into prearranged categories is not at issue. The question is what sustains Azande beliefs in oracles, what gives the oracles credibility in the first place? The answer is the same as for any system of beliefs : an array of fundamental assumptions that are never visible to the people who make them. Evans-Pritchard was sure that these capable craftsmen and farmers were not unduly swayed by emotions and that none of the then current psychological theories about magic would fit their case. In his Egyptian lectures, he described the sociological approach to belief that he intended to develop.

This is how his explanation goes: Azande could not live in the complex society they developed if their understanding of cause and effect were not the same as everyone else's. With most mishaps, they can say precisely what was the cause, whether technical incompetence or the annoyance of a powerful politician. But there is an area for curiosity that they pursue to the depths, though we Westerners leave it unplumbed. That is the ego-focused question of why any particular mishap should fall on *me* particularly. Why should two casual sequences converge so that I should happen to be in the hunting party and be in the way when the buffalo turns to gore? Why should I eat bananas every day and today eat one that disagrees with me? Why should the crumbling roof of the granary, bound to collapse one day, collapse on the day that my exposed head is there taking shade? This range of curiosity about the intersection of chains of events with my personal life is met in Azande culture by a set of prepared answers and actions. The most likely explanation is generally witchcraft. The right procedure is to consult an oracle to discover the name of the witch and then go to the accused and ask him to stop. Azande curiosity is roused (while ours is not) by the 'Why me?' question because for them it unlocks a series of institutionalized procedures by which they hold each other accountable. We have other institutions which direct curiosity differently.

The Azande were deeply preoccupied with witchcraft. But one could not say they were dominated by witchcraft fears. Witchcraft was an ordinary, everyday part of their lives. An Azande would feel the same indignation on learning that a neighbour was bewitching his affairs as we might feel on learning that a colleague had been caught embezzling. The keynote, as it were, of their system of accountability is the assumption that anyone around might deserve to be blamed for any misfortune.

So long as the offence was a minor one and could be checked, the witchcraft belief-institution had a lubricating effect on community life. Grudges would not be allowed to fester. To discover that a neighbour suspected you of harming his crops or his children was a warning to be specially considerate and polite to him. The stereotype of a witch was of a miserly, unmannerly, greedy person. To deflect accusations, Azande developed a high standard of courtesy. There was sufficient confidence in the oracle and in the neighbours to believe that a witch publicly accused was a witch stopped. Consequently next time trouble arose, or if trouble did not instantly abate, the same name would not be proposed to the oracle again. Through a prolonged series of disasters a man might confront everyone he had ever quarrelled with, one by one, and ask them to desist. This was not at all the same as asking for forgiveness. The accuser had very likely quarrelled with the accused in the past, but the oracle showed the latter to be the aggressor. The accused person was expected to perform a blessing. Good will would be restored, the air was cleared, and social life would go on.

For such beliefs to work smoothly some secondary elaborations were developed in the theory. An inherited physical substance in the body was thought to be the seat of witchcraft. A person could have it in a mild way; or it could grow powerful and so dominate his emotions that he could not keep cool control of his envy and spite. A man was more likely than a woman to be a witch. Children and young persons were more likely to be victims than attackers. The older a man grew, the stronger and more dangerous his witchcraft. This elaboration eliminated minors from the roster of plausible suspects. It is more plausible that a successful person be attacked by envious peers.

Another elaboration made it possible to accuse without causing more enmity all round. A witch could act unconsciously. This allowed a person accused by a neighbour of viciously spoiling crops or making children ill to express concerned surprise: rather like, 'My dear fellow, I had no idea, how dreadful ... I am so sorry – hey, bring the water for the blessing, I will keep a close watch so this does not happen again.' There was little ignominy in being accused:

on the contrary, since any man was likely to have witch-craft, one was grateful to be warned, as if one had a danger-ous dog or a smoking chimney. At this level of accounting for minor misfortunes, the beliefs were a way of facilitating neighbourly good relations, or at least a damper on pos-sible explosions.

However, major misfortunes must sometimes occur. Witchcraft theory also explained death and permitted ven-geance. A witch who had killed was a public danger, and the kin of this witch were expected to attend to his ex-ecution. In the old days, before the Anglo-Egyptian Con-dominium had forbidden it, a poison-ordeal administered to the accused instead of to a chicken detected and killed the guilty witch. The poison-ordeal was administered, as a branch of the judiciary, by the prince. Some people could come through the ordeal unharmed, others succumbed. The death of witches in the ordeal upheld the belief in witch-craft and in the efficacy of the ordeal. Moreover, the social demands for justice and vengeance were satisfied. If the suspect could not be brought to drink the poison, the prince's oracle would confirm (by poison given to chickens) whether he was indeed guilty and if so, gave permission for the victim's kin to spear him. At one level this would seem to be the end of the matter. But it is not the end of possible action and further justifications to which the system of belief is put. The anthropologist's enquiry goes on.

At this stage of analysis, Evans-Pritchard had shown how the local institutions were integrated with central political authority. The oracle was presented as an instrument of political control. But the Azande were highly intelligent, critical and sceptical people. A person accused and judged guilty did not necessarily accept the verdict, nor did his kin. It might be extremely inconvenient to do so. The Azande were continually testing and trying to verify their oracle. For example, according to their theory, witchcraft was inherited in the male line. If a man were speared as a witch, his sons would be proven to be genetically tainted. Their chance of rebutting accusations made against them-

selves would be better if they could show their father to
have been falsely accused and unjustly killed. Evans-
Pritchard now had another institution to explain: the
autopsy on the body of a convicted witch. It would be the
honourable duty of a dear friend of the deceased to make
the lateral gash in his side and to unwind his intestines on
a forked stick to be inspected by a team of experts. The
experts might well declare that witchcraft substance was
absent, in which case the mourners would have cleared the
name of their family and have a claim to compensation. But
the failure of the oracles would need to be explained. Not
much problem about that. Oracles were very delicate pieces
of machinery, very sensitive to contamination; any little
carelessness in protecting the poison or in purifying the
oracle-consulter would explain a mistake. Fortunately the
prince had a nearly infallible oracle. No ruler could expect
to keep 300 wives and political hegemony without an ef-
ficient intelligence system. Only the prince had both the
incentive and the means to protect the purity of his oracle.
So everyone had an incentive to bring problems to the
princely oracle. The connection between the local witchcraft idea-institution and the centralized power supported
the whole society. All the prince needed to do to control
awkward questions was to enforce secrecy about the results
of the oracle consultations.

In two pages I have summarized a system whose philosophical implications Evans-Pritchard elaborates over 500
pages. Everything works: each part contributes to the maintenance of the whole; no engines are idling. The work that
the thought does is social. After this study was published,
it should not have been possible to make philosophical statements about thought without recognizing that thought
makes cuts and connections between actions. Questions
about rationality should be questions about the coherence
of particular actions within articulated institutions.

At the time that Evans-Pritchard was there, Azande
society had undergone radical change. The princes were no
longer supreme and autonomous; their wars had stopped

and their armies were disbanded. Only a semblance of their former lives remained: their motives, risks and rewards were now set at a low level by Anglo-Egyptian Condominium. Consequently the theory and practice of witchcraft also had been adapted to new conditions. To accuse a person of witchcraft in a colonial court was forbidden, to kill a witch was a capital offence: no more poisoning and no more spearing.

The system of ideas might have changed more than it did had not the princes, still in control, made a minor adaptation of past practice. The prince's oracle now gave poison to chickens instead of to people. It had always been the infallible oracle; it was no change to bring all accusations of lethal witchcraft to court to be confirmed or rejected. It had always been *lèse majesté* to reveal the results of the prince's oracle, an offence punishable by death. Very likely it had always been the custom when asking whether a kinsman died as a victim of witchcraft to make an outward show of his innocence, whatever the prince's verdict. One would go into public mourning for the full period prescribed for an innocent death, whether it had been declared innocent or guilty; one would come out of mourning as if cleansed by the rituals and avenged by the execution of the witch. Now, instead of sometimes spearing him and sometimes poisoning the witch, the only recourse was to kill by secret magic. In the old days the corpse of the witch was proof that vengeance had been done, but now that part was more tricky.

There were gaps in the institutions which a theory of vengeance magic filled. Even if the poison oracle had ruled him no innocent victim but a witch justly killed by vengeance magic, the kin of a dead man would start an elaborate parade of his innocence. They would go to a vendor of magic, pay for it to seek out their alleged enemy and dispatch him. The magic was detective, judge of witchcraft, and executioner. The mourners would wait, scanning news of deaths in the neighbourhood, not so unreasonable as to expect their magic to act at once, but eventually consulting their oracles as to whether the latest death could be claimed by the magic they had bought. Of course they would never reveal what they had done. A dark area of institutions in which no questions could be asked or knowledge revealed kept the old system functioning – exactly as Bartlett had foreseen.

Evans-Pritchard discovered this occluded area when he worked out that if the causes of deaths were added up, everyone would be allegedly an innocent victim of witchcraft; at the same time, since every victim was also reckoned to have been avenged, the deaths from vengeance should have come near to equalling the deaths of victims. Here was a discrepancy which struck the outsider, but never worried the Azande. They could follow up any line of reasoning that had implications for action : if no action were entailed, there was no curiosity or incentive to probe further. The institutions themselves were precariously held together by fictions : the princes were no longer real princes, their status had little power. The same paste and paper that covered the cracks in the political system covered cracks in the thought system. At this stage Evans-Pritchard took a natural history approach. He worked out the taxonomy and traced the connection between the parts. But for this exercise, he would have been unable to observe a discrepancy of which insiders did not need to take note. Nor would he have been able to validate his insight that magic, like other thinking, is a vehicle of social concerns, its logic limited only by the limits of socially recognized responsibility.

The Azande had a genetic theory of witchcraft transmission. The theory was adapted so that questions about transmission were directed away from those social relationships where claims could not be collected. If witchcraft went in the male line, then it would be unwise for a son to accuse his father or a father his son, for either would imply a tainted heredity for the accuser; moreover, there was no way either could get compensation of any kind by that means from the other.

The situation is very comparable to the inhibitions against exploring genetic transmission of intelligence in our own society. Liberal thinkers back out of this possible enquiry, in horror of dubbing any part of the human race congenitally superior or inferior. Political embarrassment also inhibits such enquiry, for anyone who boldly raises the question may have awkward criticism to meet about the illiberality of his views.

So when Evans-Pritchard asked the Azande how it was that everyone did not have witchcraft in their genetic make-up, since all were intermarried, they were surprised. It seemed not to have occurred to them that it was inconsistent to go through the elaborate autopsy to clear a dead man's name and to declare one particular descent line to be clear, when by their own theory all must be equally tainted. It was not illogical of them. They had riders to the main hypothesis, which could explain why a particular person was not a witch even if his lineage was known to be a witch line. But more practically, there was much to be gained by foregrounding the genetic theory on some occasions and ignoring it on others. Thus the interlocking of institutions produces blocks to enquiry.

On the other hand, because they made witchcraft accusations, a theory of consciousness had to be elaborated in Azande thought. Other peoples who believe in witchcraft have other prophylactic measures and ways of dealing with it without naming the suspect. They often think it fatal to mention the name of a person believed to be bewitching their affairs lest the gossip makes the suspect angry enough to kill. In such a situation, if the witch is not going to be publicly accused, they can live comfortably with the idea that the witch is a fully conscious agent. But since the whole apparatus of Azande institutions for dealing with witches involved asking them to stay their dangerous actions, the institution of public accusation was made easier by the theory of unconscious witchcraft.

Then again, the theory of witchcraft, being essentially a method of pinning blame on others, had to be tailored to fit the social requirements for proper moral and technical responsibility. Individuals were held accountable in Azande society for their technical incompetence. It availed a bad craftsman nothing to claim that a witch made his tools slip. To blame witchcraft for a bad technical performance would only arouse laughter. And the same for moral responsibility : it availed an adulterer nothing to protest to the injured husband that a witch caused him to commit adultery; of course not, the Azande were too clever. One system of complaints and claims was separated from another until the area in which witchcraft was an allowable charge against someone was fully defined: it was the area of ambiguous relationships, rivalries between peers, points in their institutions where friction arises and where no buffers of social rank or wealth created distance between persons. And even in that area, the kind of disasters that could be charged to witches were limited so as not to drain personal responsibility out of the system. Here again we can talk of a system of accountability, because its boundaries are clear. All deaths except for those in war were attributed to witchcraft; it would be hopeless to pursue claims against witches behind the enemy lines, and so here the accountability system stopped again.

The complementary aspects of different kinds of claims are apparent when we find that no members of the aristocratic clan could ever be accused of witchcraft, because of an axiomatic belief that there was no witchcraft in their line of descent. This hereditary cut-off ensured that commoners would not tangle with aristocrats by accusing them of witchcraft. It also ensured that aristocrats did not accuse one another. But since their lives were full of opportunities for hatred and jealousy, another theory explained how they could do comparable harm to each other : aristocrats used sorcery, spells and magic, material substances to harm, even if they were not endowed with the witch's innate psychic powers.

When this analysis is complete, there appear to be gaps in the Azande thought system, but the institutions are integrated. The gaps in the thinking sustain the interdigitation of the institutions. Wherever there is a pressure to introduce order into social behaviour, regulatory ideas develop, but each set of regulations as it gets applied creates other areas where uncertainty needs to be reduced. To make the institutions work, new ideas are produced to fit the pieces coherently together or to sustain the credibility of the whole. The institutions are an abstraction; they have no life of their own; the pressure to organize thought introduces new entities into the universe, such as hereditary witchcraft substance in the intestines, or careful distinctions between witchcraft and non-hereditary powers of sorcery. The special Azande array of existences unknown to our world all derive from concerns to escape accountability or to hold people to account.

Naturally each Zande was more specially interested in the possibilities of holding other people accountable than in being held to account. They were bent on arguing that they and their kin were victims and their neighbours were aggressors. Their thought was dominated more by suspicion than by trust. The Nuer, by contrast, appeared to be more occupied by the conditions for sustaining a system of self-help; that is, by a concern to ensure that kin delivered reciprocal support. The two kinds of concern went with two different qualities in person-to-person dealings. One kind of social reality, built on one kind of accountability, invested fellow-humans with sinister psychic powers; the other subjected a world filled with spirits and ghosts to the will of a righteous god.

Evans-Pritchard's exercise in understanding Azande witchcraft beliefs has resounding implications for philosophy. But though the Azande are as much quoted[3] as the Bororo, one suspects that *Witchcraft, Oracles and Magic among the Azande* is not frequently read. We, in our culture, have endowed only a particular set of existences with plausibility. One of the sources of error lies in the assumption that the universes of other cultures should hold no more and no less than the entities that interest ourselves.

We should admit that we freely create new entities at need – for example, IQ, to solve social problems of competitive entry, or to absolve from legal responsibility. If we recognize that these entities are patently devised as part of our system of accountability, and that there are as many opaque areas and gaps in our curiosity about them as the Azande have about their witches and demons, then Evans-Pritchard's lesson will have struck home.

Here we may pose a recurring question of sociological method and objectivity. Imported assumptions distort the interpretation of evidence. It is not difficult to make objectively valid statements about the Azande government. The role of prince is physically defined by habitation and clothing, as well as by the pattern of footsteps on the ground. But when it comes to their ideas about witchcraft one has to be careful. It is legitimate to ask how Azande witchcraft ideas intermesh with Azande political ideas, and how Azande witchcraft institutions relate to Azande political institutions, however these may be consistently defined. But to ask how these ideas affect institutions implies that the ideas have a life of their own and can be observed influencing the institutions – whereas, in all cases it is people who have ideas and who influence institutions. An expectation that ideas can somehow be mapped out apart from the institutions in which they work is similarly misleading. Again, to present the general relation between ideas and institutions as a feasible field of enquiry, leaving out the persons and intentions that generate both, is another form of the general fallacy. It is as if a neurologist were to claim to investigate mind and matter, when all he is capable of doing is tracing which parts of the brain control which neural systems, always recognizing that this alleged brain control is proved by particular movements in the body.

Of course the larger overview is necessary and should be undertaken by everyone, all the time, and not only by qualified metaphysicians. Sherrington conducted this generalizing exercise, when he wrote a popular and highly influential book on *Man on His Nature* (1953). The general enquiry of where we are now should not be shirked. But it should be conducted, as Sherrington conducted his, within a frankly metaphysical frame of reference. Within the authoritative framework of sociological enquiry the arbitrary separation of ideas from the institutions in which they work creates a pernicious dichotomy, as if mind were out there, an existence, disembodied, supported by nothing, but somehow powerfully influencing the solidly physical institutions in curious ways. This perspective allows insoluble questions to fill the central forum of sociological debate.

6. Accountability among the Nuer

The fieldwork remove from Azande to Nuer forced an extra-ordinary awareness on Evans-Pritchard. He was already very sensitive to methodological problems. Working through the magical beliefs of the Azande and coming out the other side with a full account of their rationality, through correct chains of inference to the underlying assumptions and from these to their plausibility as embodied in social institutions, he was alert to the pitfalls. Before he published *Witchcraft, Oracles and Magic among the Azande* in 1937, he had already finished his Nuer fieldwork. The two intense experiences lived side by side in his mind while he wrote the first book.

It is possible to describe Azande institutional life and the distribution of power and, in discussing their system of thought, to map the parts of each upon the other. Rudimentary in some cases and hypertrophied in others, their social institutions can be transposed to our own view of the main divisions of social life; the family, local government, judiciary, military and governmental functions had their obvious distinctive counterparts. Not so with the Nuer. The style of Nuer life at once reveals the local limitations of our categories. Their institutions are invisible. Every now and again a regulatory idea surfaces and marshalls activity, then sinks out of sight, while another becomes visible in its effect upon movements of cattle and people. If they can be said to have anything corresponding to political institutions, these have absolutely no physical form, no architecture of palaces or prisons, no embodiment in piles of stones – not even any territorial divisions except those made by natural features such as rivers, watering little communities separated by drier land from the others. Even the verbal grading of different sociological levels is absent : the Nuer word for 'lineage' is used at every level, so that the biggest tribe and all its constituent units are called by the same term. Anyone already alert to false abstractions and careless imposing of ideas from one culture to another would meet here the perfect challenge to make a new beginning.

We should distinguish two senses in which the word 'system' is used in the social sciences. The commonsense use of 'system' refers to a set of relationships such that all parts contribute to the maintenance of the whole. If one element is changed, then because of their systematic connection all will be transformed. The main interest here is the taxonomic interconnections. A tribe undergoing industrial/colonial pressures may start to grow cash-crops; the task of the anthropologist examining the social system is to trace how the one or two changes in technology affect the economy, family, life and religion, etc. At this rather simple level of theory, it is usual to assume that something about the inter-relation of the parts ensures also that when one element is altered, there is still some power to return to the original pattern, a homeostatic assumption. It makes sense to assert that a principle of stability must be there if the society seems to endure minor changes and resist major ones. But saying that there is homeostatis is not to explain how it works.

The other usage of the word 'system' focuses directly upon homeostatic principles. The work of the investigator is to identify how the stabilizing controls work. Norbert Wiener, who has already appeared in this book as the young man who gave Frederick Bartlett an idea about how to experiment with memory, founded the branch of science called cybernetics; a cybernetic control mechanism is one in which the system's inputs turn themselves off and on again so that a given state is maintained at the level set by the controls. The thermostatic oven is a familiar example. Wiener developed his idea to explain how living organisms maintain a regular body temperature. He also applied it to many other systems.

Evans-Pritchard presented the Nuer political system in terms of feedback. He described the inputs and the regulatory mechanism; the output was the political system maintained at a certain level of assured safety for life, limb and property. He worked out the model because there was nothing else to use from existing political theory or anthropology to explain an ordered society kept in being without the exercise of centralized, coercive power.

The Azande political stage is filled with princes, governors, deputies, aristocrats and commoners, mutilated convicts, rich men, poor men, and many other social statuses that can be mapped on to territorial fields of responsibility. But the Nuer political scene is sparse, practically empty.

The social life of the Nuer is strongly regulated. Every man knows what is due to him. A tally of compensation for insults and injuries is known, any transaction in rights is affirmed by a corresponding transfer of livestock. If a debtor fails to pay, his creditor can walk into a strange camp, unhitch a beast of corresponding value, and safely walk away with it, no friends of the debtor lifting a finger to harm or stop him. Nuer women can move safely about, enjoying much greater respect and freedom than Azande women. Regulation is there, but power is diffused through the whole system. Each man has to defend his own rights.

Many tribes are organized on principles that seem to be of this self-help kind, but when there is really a free-for-all, the strongest wins, and contests of individual strength are daily events. The elementary principle of self-help usually produces great disparities of wealth and power. But here, with the Nuer, the strongest does not win. There is little accumulation of wealth. The cattle, goats and sheep are evenly distributed among households. There is no accumulation of power. The phrase 'ordered anarchy' seems to describe the situation. There is no social contract, no agreement to limit individual liberties so as to allow power to accumulate with one or two people for the sake of the good order.

The regulation has to be analysed at three levels: first, the diffusion of power over balanced segments of the tribe; second, the maintenance of the balance; third, the thought system that values each individual self and makes a frame by which self can be transcended. Only this third analysis reveals the switch control for the political feedback system.

The phrase 'structural opposition' summarizes the system by which power is diffused throughout the Nuer tribe. All the units of the society are divided according to clearly known orders of magnitude. At the highest level, the whole tribe divides into two or possibly three sections; then each of these divides again, and these again and again, until the smallest political units, the local communities, are reached. The local neighbourhoods, containing several villages, are usually self-sufficient in seasonal resources. Within a village everyone counts as kin. At the next inclusive level, within a local community, there is a sense of common interest, more quarrelling and sharing, than between communities. A quarrel with people in far distant communities is less likely, for the more people have to do with each other, the more cause there is for quarrelling. When a Nuer feels insulted or wronged, he does not take advice or seek arbitration.

> He at once challenges the man who has wronged him to a duel and the challenge must be accepted. There is no other way of settling a dispute and a man's courage is his only protection against aggression ... From their earliest years children are encouraged by their elders to settle all disputes by fighting, and they grow up to regard skill in fighting the most necessary accomplishment and courage the highest virtue.
>
> Boys will fight with spiked bracelets. Men of the same village or camp fight with clubs, for it is a convention that spears must not be used between close neighbours lest one of them be killed and the community be split by a blood-feud. It is also a convention that no third person may take part in the fight, even though he be a close kinsman of one of the combatants. Once a fight has begun neither party can give way and they have to continue till one or the other is badly injured unless, as generally happens, people pull them away from each

other, loudly protesting, and then stand between them.

When a fight starts between persons of different villages it is with the spear; every adult male of both communities takes part in it; and it cannot be stopped before considerable loss of life has ensued. Nuer know this and, unless they are very angry, are reluctant to start a fight with a neighbouring village.[1]

This first superficial stage of Evans-Pritchard's analysis reveals the lines of cleavage along which Nuer hostilities flare up and are damped. The tribe is divided into segments, each of which has many characteristics of the tribe itself :

Each has its distinctive name, its comon sentiment, and its unique territory ... so that the spatial divisions of the rains are maintained and may be accentuated during the drought ... The smaller the tribal segment, the more compact its territory, the more contiguous its members, the more varied and intimate their social ties, and the stronger therefore its sentiment of unity ...[2]

The first elementary principle of their organization is that political cohesion varies with variations of political distance and is also a function of structural distance in genealogical terms. The second is that each segment is further segmented. The third is that there is opposition between all the segmented parts. Members of any segment unite for wars against adjacent segments of the same order and unite with these adjacent segments against larger sections. These principles combine to make a political system founded upon the structural opposition of its parts. Every status and claim to loyalty is relative to the whole : at any point in time, the structural distance between opponents determines the constellation of enemies and allies, and this can change at any other point in time. At one time a small unit splits, at another time it fuses with its opponent against a larger foe. The continuous fission and fusion follow the predictable lines of structural distance. Evans-Pritchard had to call it structural distance, because though it has a geographical basis, geography does not fully describe its mobilizing effects, and though it has a connection with kinship, kinship does not either explain how the land is divided up.

Hints of Einsteinian relativism colour Evans-Pritchard's language here, and more than a hint of biological analogy. We should recall Sherrington's principle of reciprocal opposition and reinforcement in the nervous system. This Nuer political system is described by Evans-Pritchard as if the segments were moved by muscles that had power mutually to support or inhibit:

> Feuds are settled with comparative ease in a restricted social milieu where the structural distance between the participants is narrow, but they are more difficult to settle as the milieu expands, until one reaches the inter-tribal boundaries, where no compensation is offered or expected. The degree of social control over feuds varies with the size of the tribal segment, and Nuer themselves have often tried to explain this to me.[3]

The boundaries of the system are determined by the boundaries of the intention to treat all Nuer by the same rules. The force of law is not the same for all Nuer, but weakens with the structural distance between parties to a dispute. At the outer edges the will to deal justly with all Nuer, even if it were there, is checked by natural obstacles, physical distance, empty bushland, and the need to travel.

> The larger the segment involved the greater the anarchy that prevails. People say that there is payment of blood-cattle between primary sections, but they do not greatly feel the need of paying it. The tribe is the last stage in this increasing anarchy. It still has nominal unity ... If many men are killed in a big fight between large sections, nothing is done to avenge them or pay compensation for their deaths. Their kinsmen bide their time until there is another fight. The political integument may in consequence

be stretched eventually to the breaking-point and the tribe split into two.[4]

The second general characteristic of the Nuer political system is that its boundaries are created by logistic failure not by foreign treaty. Political will and the rule of law just fade out at the edges of the system. For the Nuer, the boundaries of their system are the natural limits of law and order. Furthermore, in the sociology of knowledge to which their example contributes, the boundaries of their polity are the limits of their knowledge. The fact that there is a known boundary enables their thought to reach out to the edges, and move back in curling waves of analogy, folding one situation upon another so that the match of metaphors is irresistible. By knowing how their social system is bounded they bound the possibilities of their knowledge system. Then they establish truth and understanding within it by innumerable proofs and demonstrations.

So much for the first point, the diffusion of power by structural opposition; so far Evans-Pritchard has given no account of the principles of self-regulation, only a very convincing account of balance achieved through countervailing forces. Even at this stage it sounds seductively complete, so that one is tempted to be satisfied here, and not to ask how the opposing units in the Nuer structure are so well-marked that balance is sustained, or to ask whether this is really the case or whether some other mechanism still needs to be uncovered. One might mention that most anthropologists, describing a political system, bring their own enquiry to rest when they have shown a balance of forces.

At the next stage of questioning, Evans-Pritchard described the feedbacks. The inputs to the political system were the obligation to fight and the principle of descent through males that aligns real or fictive brothers, but forbids brothers (as situationally defined) to fight against each other. The control mechanism combines the feud, the possibility of paying blood compensation instead of taking a life for a life, and the theory that homicide pollutes the earth. No honourable man would accept cattle in place of a slain brother, but human bloodshed pollutes the earth so that whole communities are endangered : if the kin of the slayer were to drink or eat with the kin of the victim, they would all die from the contamination of blood. Nothing would save them except religious sacrifice to wipe out the pollution. The effect of this theory is to bring great pressure to bear upon disputing parties if they live in the same village or even in the same neighbourhood, for all the people who drink the same river water are placed at risk, all being kin to one or both parties. The fear of pollution of blood fades out beyond the local community and is totally ineffective where structural and geographical distances decrease the risks of shared water resources. The pollution theory is nicely adjusted to political realities. It gives the local doves some leverage against the hawks, obliging them to swallow their pride, accept forty head of cattle (no mean amount), and save the community from epidemic.

Insofar as a feud cannot be settled peacefully between distant segments, each new outbreak of killing defines the lines between them – a Durkheimian point. Insofar as blood pollution theory brings truce and peace, it does so in the places where kinship and local loyalties are strong. The theory is credible because it fits the institutions. The feud maintains the structural opposition, defines the units, identifies the areas of lasting solidarity. Each time the internal opposition by which the system maintains itself rises to the point of blood being shed, the latent hostility within the smallest units is damped by pollution fears. 'The likelihood of a homicide developing into a blood-feud, its force, and its chances of settlement are thus dependent on the structural interrelations of the persons concerned.'[5]

To complete the analysis, the anthropologist has to delve further into the thought system which channels personal pride to the defence of political boundaries. Nuer pride reaches extraordinary heights.

The ordered anarchy in which they live accords well with their character, for it is impossible to live among Nuer and conceive of rulers ruling over them. The Nuer is a product of hard and egalitarian upbringing, is deeply democratic, and is easily roused to violence. His turbulent spirit finds any restraint irksome and no man recognizes a superior ... That every Nuer considers himself as good as his neighbour is evident in their every movement. They strut about like lords of the earth, which, indeed, they consider themselves to be. There is no master and no servant in their society, but only equals who regard themselves as God's noblest creation. Their respect for one another contrasts with their contempt for all other peoples. Among themselves even the suspicion of an order riles a man and either he does not carry it out or he carries it out in a casual and dilatory manner that is more insulting than a refusal.[6]

Why is pollution of blood such a fearful thing to Nuer that it can constrain their pride and end a feud? The Nuer hold themselves in a tension of pride and humility : the pride is in their superiority to every other person, the humility derives from their habit of reflecting deeply on the human condition and on their relation to God. Continually the relativity of their moral code places them in ambiguous and conflicting situations. They must fight, they must not shed blood : this is an example of the moral knife-edge on which they continually walk, their daily lives hedged with rules which circumstances inevitably lead them to break. No wonder they say that man is bound to commit faults, that faults accumulate without the offender's being aware of what he has done.

To meet these double pulls of moral consciousness they have worked out complex exonerations and remissions, with fine distinctions between accidental and intentional wrong-doing, faults graded from big to small. Keeping all these reflections in suspense, to the advantage of clear decision they gather them into a single strong theory of God, sin, expiation and forgiveness achieved by sacrifice. Pollution of the earth by bloodshed would hardly be a credible danger if it did not figure in a list of many other sins regularly seen to entail illness and death if not expiated. Their commitment to a theory of sin and of its consequences is the ontological anchorage for the control mechanism of Nuer political life. Equivalent to the Azande theory of witchcraft, the Nuer theory of sin is the touchstone of reality to which all their elaborate legal fictions relate.

Some of the threads of Evans-Pritchard's argument can now be drawn together. The foundation of meaning, according to my reconstruction upon his work, is the system of accountability. As people decide to hold others accountable, and as they allow the same principles to extend universally, even to apply to themselves, they set up a particular kind of moral environment for each other. According to the pressures created by this environment the mind's thought is discriminated and toughened. The Nuer hold others totally accountable; they must be prepared to die and prepared to kill. They expect themselves to be held equally accountable. The price is so high that they notch up detailed tallies of mutual accountability and split logical hairs with the gusto of medieval casuists, to establish precise obligations. Their commitment to their system of accountability gives them the incentive to work out the fullest exegesis of their principles. Surely no Talmudists excel the Nuer in establishing the string of consequences entailed by principles. For the anthropologist's purpose they were even better fitted than the Azande to demonstrate the powers of hard reasoning active in primitive society.

Evans-Pritchard's fieldwork method required him to support everything he said with evidence drawn from observation, the evidence that would be squeezed out of greetings and quarrels and especially from reaction to misfortune. He tried never to declare a belief or theory not supported by action. The deed explains the principle as much as the principle explains the deed.

A test case arises with the word 'idiom', one of his

favourite terms for discussing Nuer political organization.
He calls a principle an idiom, when although appealed to
locally as if a description, it is in no way an accurate
description of what is happening. The idiom of descent
through the male line is a way of thinking about political
relations; it provides a conceptual framework for political
organization; it is a way of thinking about the relation
between political units 'as though'[7] it were a relation between kinsmen, *as though* the tribe were a genealogical
system, *as though* the local community were identical with
a lineage it was named after. Usually, when idiom or
ideology is used to explain social behaviour, no other explanation is available. The idiom, instead of being merely
a local medium of description, is treated as an explanation
in itself.

Why do they do this or this? For ideological reasons or
because they think in this idiom.[8] When Evans-Pritchard
writes in this vein, is there not a falling off from the strict
positivist ideal on which he assembles his evidence? Why
can he not drop the idiom and say that the lineage is identical with the local community, and that the local communities are connected with each other by ties of male
descent? He cannot, because it is not true. Nuer lineages are
not corporate, localized communities. They are dispersed
and mixed up together. His census did not produce any
picture of a system of genealogical relationships connecting
male relatives with each other and local units linked with
each other, as descendants of brothers, or sons and fathers.
Nuer move freely over the land and settle where they please.
The real units in the political system are villages and their
local communities. This being so, any sceptic is at liberty to
ask for the evidence of this alleged idiom of descent in the
male line.

But Evans-Pritchard very carefully assembled evidence for
the many shared commitments to legal fictions by which
Nuer social life is maintained. Lineage has little reality as a
residential unit; like other social institutions, among the
Nuer the lineage emerges at specific occasions, for example

at sacrifices when its members travel a long way to be together. It emerges clearly at feasts and distributions of cattle. As a residential principle, no; as an active principle of organization for wealth-holding the evidence is convincing that this idiom is more than a way of thinking about institutions, it is a way of organizing them within the local communities. Between community neighbourhoods the politics of fission and fusion among balanced segments work entirely through the categories of descent in the male line.

The political institutions of the Nuer have special interest for the sociology of knowledge. Their institutions successively and momentarily appear in their actions and disappear, leaving no physical traces. Political life never entails contributing to the upkeep of roads and bridges or paying a levy to a leader. They do not build a court house or even a pillory. This is part of the extraordinary attraction of these people : whatever political principles exist are maintained entirely in their minds. The feedback of the political system works within the system of thought. Nuer hold each other accountable according to ideas of lineage affiliation. They have certain clear ideas about what it is to be in the right, and they agree that most Nuer are most of the time at fault. Somewhere in their ideas about what can go wrong and how to set it right, a whole social system is evolved, negative feedbacks and all.

The model is well enough explained. If it be correctly understood, it can illuminate a central problem in philosophy. That thought is embedded in institutions has been established. Now it is a matter of asking what kinds of thoughts and what kinds of institutions. From this example we can compare accountability systems to offer fresh answers to the old questions. From here on I shall assume that whatever can be said about a belief as belonging to a system implies the same about the relevant social institution, since each only lives in the other.

7. Reasoning and Memory

Individuals vary greatly in their capacity to recall past experiences. Once, psychologists treated memory as if it were an isolated faculty of the mind of which the most conclusive tests would measure the capacity to retain and reproduce arbitrary strings of information.[1] It would take away from the high marks that could be scored to the credit of pure memory if the subject had some interest in the topic or if the items made some sort of sense to him. Against this trend of experimental work, which was not producing impressive results, Bartlett had entered the contrary idea that memory is directly influenced by social factors. We have seen that he did not succeed in devising tests that would go beyond this affirmation. But when he wrote that social conditions control individual recall 'by providing that setting of interest, excitement and emotion which follows the development of specific images and socially by providing a persistent framework of restrictions and customs which acts as a schematic basis for constructive memory,'[2] he had wished to introduce a new approach to experimental psychology.

Alas for Bartlett that he did not understand better what Maurice Halbwachs was trying to do on the self-same subject. A pupil of Henri Bergson, of Durkheim and of Mauss, Halbwachs took for his main research project to demonstrate that perception and recall depend primarily upon social institutions and secondly upon physical, visible symbols.[3]

In Durkheim's theory of religion the totem is an emblem which serves by its physical existence to fix an otherwise fleeting, abstract idea. If it were not for this physical existence as a point of reference, ideas about religion would have no stability. Secondly, for Durkheim's theory, religious ideas are particularly vulnerable to destabilizing forces because they are second-remove ideas about another abstraction, society itself. They depend on social commitment. Insofar as the individual has a commitment to society, that commitment has to be hedged around with physical markings, rules of taboo. The concept of society as having overriding authority is transformed into a concept of Godhead.

Halbwachs's contribution is to work out in detail the social and physical supports of memory. The temporal stages of an event are more easily recalled if they can be given a spatial ordering that corresponds to the temporal sequence. Concern to establish the social framework of memory leads him to discuss the different memory of different social classes, pegged out by different physical memorials. Instead of considering the spatial layout of Australian camps or the seasonal movements of the Eskimos, as Durkheim and Mauss had done, he applied himself to European history and contemporary life. He was particularly interested in the negative case of how memory could be sustained without that spatial structure that seemed to be its prerequisite, in the same way as Durkheim had taught that religious organization has an inherent problem of cognitive stability unless it takes over a spatial anchorage.

Evans-Pritchard's work on reasoning and remembering derived from this double heritage : the English psychologist's interest in the institutional frameworks that sustain memory, and the French sociologist's researches in the same direction. He presented Nuer social institutions as the schematic framework of memory. Whenever the Nuer seek to clarify the definition of a status, they state it in terms of claims to cattle. The intense emotional value of cattle in Nuer imagination and poetry should not be overlooked. Lines of relationships, so complex to the outsider to unravel, would be crystal clear and easy to recall to the person who stands to gain a cow or an ox from correctly computing them. Nuer social life illustrates how an individual's powers of retention and retrieval of information are stimulated by social factors. There are rewards for recognizing sharp distinctions and penalties for forgetting them. So

keenness of individual perception is encouraged along prescribed lines. Memory will be continually revived by occasions on which claims would be contested and honoured.
Each wedding and funeral is an occasion for claims and
counter-claims, to say nothing of the major crises of loyalty
in fighting. Attention is strongly focused on distinctions
used as principles for distributing wealth.

A set of questions arises about the social stimulus to
logical discrimination. How social life selectively focuses
attention and jogs memory is important in itself. Just because attention is selective, gaps in knowledge inevitably
appear. The Azande case illustrates institutionalized blocks
to curiosity. The Nuer studies further illustrate principles of
rejection which automatically send some information to
oblivion. They also provide a complex example of benchmarks used to organize time past, by which historical series
are grouped for retrieval. Since this work contributes to a
central element in Marxist theory, that is the relation between superstructure and infrastructure, I am always surprised that self-styled Marxist anthropologists pay it so little
attention – perhaps an institutional-ideological focus blocks
curiosity.

First let me set the question of logical discrimination back
into its old anthropological context. Recall that there are
still extant societies that have no words for counting beyond
the number three, and others in which four or seven is the
limit of the numerate skills. Apparently people with no
worldly possessions worth counting can manage quite comfortably with a linguistic competence for distinguishing
numbers only up to three. Asked, 'How many of your
children are living with you?' a mother with six around
her knees will feel content to reply something like 'a lot' or
'many' or 'all these'. This does not mean she cannot name
them all in order of birth or notice when one is missing.
Judgement of quantities is an even more complex matter.
Some shepherds are said to scan a large flock of sheep and
register how many and which are absent in much less time
than it would take to count them. However, a hundred

years ago it was naturally tempting to consider these non-numerates as simple children of nature, and to try to work out a social developmental sequence that parallelled that of the stages in which children learn to count. The implications of ranging such societies on a series from most infantile to more numerate were never tested because extraordinary discrepancies in the capacities for reckoning, judgement and memory rendered any single grading criterion useless. Some people whose technology might cause them to be placed at a primitive stage performed prodigious feats of memory when it came to reciting genealogies of kings or ancestors. The idea came to be accepted that primitive peoples were good at learning by rote and that their best remembering was the result of mechanical mnemonics.

Bartlett thought that a strong social support to memory was inclined to produce a mechanical style of recall. His idea was that when the social institutions provided the mnemonic setting, recall was of the recitative type; by contrast, when an individual, free from the guidance and constraints of his society, had to remember, he did so with 'none of that relatively effortless, recitative, copying manner which marked the recall of the native. The plan was built up bit by bit, a detail here, a filling up there, then another key and so on. The whole process had every appearance of a genuine construction.'[4]

The idea that institutions are something which the primitive takes as given – a fixed, unalterable part of his environment – dies hard. It is one of the sources of a theoretical division between ourselves, modern industrial man, thought to be free of tradition's grip, free to argue the toss and exert our influence over institutions, and they, the primitives, who are supposed to accept the encrusted yoke of custom. Evans-Pritchard demonstrated how they, too, negotiate their claims and construct their culture in doing so. He did it by entering into the way that the Nuer use their principles of discrimination.

In the perennial controversy about human behaviour and its psychological basis, prohibitions on incest are often discussed. Sometimes it is argued that humans have a natural aversion to sexual congress with close kin, in which case the rules they observe are not intellectual constructions but instinctive responses. The counter-argument rests on the observation that humans are frequently not deterred by the alleged instinctive aversion : humans seem to be no different from animals in their readiness to mate with kin; and on this argument, social considerations explain the prevalence and form of such regulations. Nuer theory comes down unequivocally on the side of a sociological explanation of incest regulation. Nuer say that it is unthinkable for a mother and son to have sexual relations. The whole context for this unthinkability is laid out by their justification of the regulations in less heinous cases. Basically sex and marriage are organized by the transfer of cattle. Cattle-givers cannot give cattle to themselves, so the elementary requirements of a transaction draw a boundary around kin who hold common rights as cattle claimants. Every prohibited relationship is forbidden explicitly 'because of the cattle'. The regulation is on a par with our law which disallows evidence given in court by a wife against or for her husband.

Nuer incest regulations are as follows. Marriage is forbidden between clansfolk – relationships traced in the male line. It is forbidden also between a man and a woman related through either father or mother (by male or female links) up to six generations. It is forbidden between close natural kinsfolk, that is, between persons related through sexual union outside of marriage; for example, a man could not marry the daughter of his maternal grandfather's natural son. Thus far the rules would seem to be concentrated on closeness of biological relationship, and might support the theory that an instinct is being codified into laws. But adoption is also a bar to intermarriage. A captured boy of the Dinka tribe, if adopted by his captors, counts as a son, and he cannot marry into their lineage. Even if he be adopted into a different lineage from that of his captors, men from his captor's lineage are forbidden to marry his daughter. The reason given is the same kind given in all cases: when the Dinka boy marries, his captors will contribute cattle to the marriage payments for his wife, which gives them a claim to some of the cattle that will come in when his daughter eventually marries; it is impossible for them to marry a girl at whose marriage they are entitled to claim cattle: it would be an incestuous union. The rule by which they forego sex gives them a claim to the cows due to kinsfolk. Only if there were no recognized relationship can they have sexual intercourse or marry. When a captured Dinka girl is adopted, her adoptive kin perform a religious rite and say, 'She will become our daughter and we will receive her bridewealth cattle.' The cattle of her bridewealth give her kinship, and with it the right to receive the cows due to the paternal aunt on the marriage of her captor's sons. Marriage is forbidden between her descendants and the descendants of those kinsmen in virtue of her bridewealth for several generations. Nuer state all the rules in terms of rights to cattle. The transfers of cattle create the close relationships that are incompatible with marriage.

The fact that a man cannot marry his wife's sister, or any near kinswoman of his wife, as second wife unless the first wife has died without children, is also explained in terms of cattle. 'When your daughter is married her mother's sister is entitled to a cow of her bridewealth, and Nuer hold that she cannot both receive this cow and be your wife at the same time, especially as the cow is in some degree regarded as part of the bridewealth still owing from your marriage to your wife.' The rules against marrying the daughter of an age-mate give an even clearer acknowledgement of the social nature of the prohibition.

The blood age-mates have shed together into the ground at their initiation gives them a kind of kinship. In certain circumstances an age-mate may claim a cow ... of the bridewealth of the daughter of one of his mates and a man may not be in the position of paying bridewealth and being able to claim it. Nuer point out also that were a man to marry the daughter of an age-mate her parents would become his parents-in-law, and the respect he would have to show them would be incompatible with the familiarity with which he should treat age-mates and their wives and the liberties he may take with them. He could not, for instance, eat and drink in their home, an abstention in glaring contradiction to the behaviour expected of age-mates.[5]

Very evidently the Nuer divides his social universe into kin and not-kin. From male kin he expects support in fighting, vengeance if he is killed, and cattle distribution when kinswomen are married. Kinship means claims on cattle. Every wedding is an occasion for reviving memories of possible claims and so reviving the lines of relationship in people's minds.[6]

To state a claim on cattle is to divide the whole universe of possible relationships into two mutually exclusive spheres of claims: 'Where the women are, the cattle are not.' Either sex claims are possible or cattle claims, but both simultaneously are impossible.

If this does not begin to illustrate the relentless demands of social accountability upon logic, a further glance at Nuer marriage will convince. Nothing gives more zest to drawing fine logical distinctions than the need to distinguish among competing claims. But the desire to reconcile incompatible situations is another powerful stimulus to logical exercise. A person wants to hold, and yet to have the credit of giving away; to enjoy sexual adventures himself while allowing no one to disrupt his own marriage; to let an unfaithful wife go away, but to claim all her offspring. Basically the Nuer want to have a social system in which rights are transmitted through wedlock, and at the same time not to constrain their womenfolk. Compared with Azande women, Nuer women enjoy great freedom and dignity. Nearly all the categories in the social system are generated through the marriage bond. Yet a Nuer woman is not forced to stay with a husband she dislikes. The Nuer reconcile potentially opposed patterns of behaviour by a series of legal fictions.

Starting from the principle that a legal marriage is established by the transfer of cattle, they pursue this principle through all the ramifications they desire.

Technically, so long as the cattle are not returned (and this is exceedingly difficult after they have been distributed to kin), a marriage endures. The mere fact that the husband dies does not end the marriage, for he has paid over the cattle once and for all. So with no new marriage being required, the widow should normally co-habit with one of her husband's brothers. Any children begotten are still to be counted as the children of the dead man. What if she might not consent to live with any of the brothers of her late husband? The brothers whom she rejects do not try to force her to stay with them against her wishes. If she wants to go away and live with a man outside their group, she can, but the children she might bear to him are still legally the children of the man who paid the cattle. If the natural father wants to legitimate his children, he only has to pay the appropriate amount of cattle. He has a material interest in doing so, for the payment entitles him to claim cows as a father at the marriage of his own daughters. If it should happen that a girl is too promiscuous to be able to settle down to marriage, her father, not having received cattle for her, can claim the children for his lineage.

The most ingenious elaboration of this legal principle is applied to the Nuer sentiment that no man should die without leaving legitimate descendants to carry on his name. If this should happen, his kinsmen are duty-bound to collect cattle and to use them to marry a woman to the dead man. His brother or nephew would normally take on the responsibility of begetting children whose place in the lineage genealogy would be as the dead man's offspring.

Looking at a Nuer village, with the identical homesteads and cattle kraals, it would be impossible to disentangle the elaborate skein of relationships between living and dead. A roster of the living men would not give all the fathers of babies being born. Dead persons are legally active, so much so that a man might inherit the widows of one brother and

E-P –D

marry a girl to the name of another, and then, having piously begotten many children to the name of dead men, might die leaving no legitimate issue to carry on his own name. Then of course the altruistic obligation to marry a woman for his ghost falls on someone else – and so on.

The honouring of this obligation has another aspect. Individual Nuer have to be ready to defend their rights with force. They risk maiming or death when they start a fight. The confidence that kinsmen would not let your name be forgotten sets a limit on the social dangers – if one can separate the physical risks from social risks. Fear of what would happen to his family and his own good name would not stop a man from laying his life on the line: the family would be cared for, and his name avenged and perpetuated. The system of accounting has to provide the conditions for its own smooth working at any level – psychological, intellectual and institutional. The Nuer find their way through this web of legal fictions because of the simple rule that they can either marry or claim cattle and kinship. This rule working in every sexual confrontation makes it easy for Nuer to see the tribe as a single genealogical system. It also means that every possible sexual adventure is an occasion on which the relationship system has to be reviewed and its principles reaffirmed.

Thus did Evans-Pritchard show how problems about accountability develop muscle in the human faculties of reasoning. The joint effort of creating Nuer society also produces a powerful machinery for turning social dilemmas into legalistic issues, solved by fictions. But important though this was, it was not quite the big discovery that psychologists in Bartlett's day would have needed to put them on another trail of enquiry. The main interest to them should have been Evans-Pritchard's analysis of how consciousness itself is structured.

Two approaches to this problem may be mentioned: one was according to the idea that the individual does his own work of accountability, sifting information and organizing it upon a personal evolving scheme, his social interests being his guide (this approximates to Bartlett's assumptions); the other (Halbwachs's), within the French sociological tradition, took more deliberate account of social pressures and of physical aids to support the meanings. Neither approach invites one to think of the blanks in memory as being social constructs, nor did they suggest that the gaps over which recall is impossible are more than a mere incidental result of the structuring of attention by social interests. Yet amnesic blanks are a crucial part of the social structuring, one of the conditions of its smooth working. However, in the 1920s no one transferred to sociology Freud's insight that some forgetfulness in the individual is a blessed help to sanity. Evans-Pritchard achieved this parallel insight for the working of the social system. By so doing he anticipated contemporary work, such as Michel Foucault's, on socially constructed oblivion. He also cut the theory of memory free from physical props.

As he saw it, the Nuer articulate their experience of past time and anchor its several parts into the articulated society on which they focus attention. Most Nuer tribes have a history of only ten or eleven generations. There is good reason to think they have been in existence as tribes in that location much longer. As the tribe is thought of by Nuer as a genealogical structure, the anthropologist was bound to ask why the succeeding generations of the dead do not cumulatively lengthen the genealogical tree.

The answer in Evans-Pritchard's work is the concept of structural distance. Every Nuer can place himself genealogically in the tribe for two kinds of purposes: for calculating political alignment, and for calculating sex and cattle trade-offs. Political alignment is determined by considering the major territorial divisions of the tribe, and the skeletal spread through them of the dominant clan. A tribe does not contain more than five or six levels of segmentation, from the most inclusive to the smallest local community. At the edges of the tribe the force of law runs out. Within each of its major divisions redress for wrongs becomes progressively easier until the last level, the local community, which is like a close-knit kinship unit. The first four or five generations of the tribe's existence from its founder to the more recently dead are continually commemorated in all the political confrontations in which a person has to assess wrongs as redressable or not. Structural distance being an active political principle, there is no difficulty in understanding how Nuer manage to remember the major levels of segmentation.

The other context for reckoning genealogy is the taking of women in marriage and the claiming and paying of cattle. In this context the reckoning of descent starts from the opposite direction. Any adult can easily recall the relationships of his father's father's father; there will be people alive and around who can corroborate. A descendant of the father's father's father may turn up at a girl's marriage and claim a calf. It would be given to him as a sign that the limit of claims has been reached, at the fourth generation. Relatives who claim relationship up to six or seven generations back would not be refused a gift; but the main genealogical structure recognized cattle claims up to and not including the fifth generation. Anyone who knows that this is how he is related, also knows that sexual intercourse with the range of girls thus defined as kin would count as incestuous.

By using one system for reckoning forwards from the beginning of time and another for reckoning backwards from the present day, the Nuer limit their historical experience. An amnesic space in the middle of the genealogy swallows up the new generations as the dead great-great-grandfathers are succeeded by new great-grandfathers. Thanks to this structural fault in the method of reckoning, an empty hole was created. Its absorbent properties reduce the whole known past and allow it to be articulated. If every generation were included, the impossible task of remembering everything would strain the cognitive schema. Lapses of memory would be individual and fortuitous instead of social and regular. The public structuring of the consciousness of time allowed the Nuer to take full cognizance of a short historical depth. The tree under which mankind came into being was still standing in western Nuerland until a few years before the research began.

The most important sentence in which Evans-Pritchard summed up the Nuer consciousness of time is : 'Beyond the annual cycle, time-reckoning is a conceptualization of the social structure, and the points for reference are a projection into the past of actual relationships between persons.' He did not consider the material benchmarks of time's passing as so vitally important for sustaining memory. The hooves treading out paths over the land as cattle are driven from one homestead to another are material aids to memory, no doubt, but they would never take it very far back. There are no written constitutions, no enduring monuments, no scenes of battle or palace ruins. The maximum historical depth is achieved by the exigencies of the Nuer social structure : 'Time is not a continuum, but is a constant structural relationship between two points, the first and last persons in a line of agnatic descent.'[7]

These statements expand easily into a testable general hypothesis and a programme for relating historical consciousness to social structure. If the Nuer case, which Evans-Pritchard demonstrated, has wider implications, then other people too use their conceptualizing of the social structure to give points of reference for projection into the past of actual social relations. Immediately after the Second World War, younger anthropologists took up this challenge. Evans-Pritchard had not explained the steps by which the present is projected into the past. Nor did he himself attempt the comparative studies which would test the general applicability of the idea. The first exercise was performed by intensive fieldwork among the Tiv of south-east Nigeria. A whole process of clipping, eliding and openly adjusting genealogies so that history would accord with the current distribution of authority was described in a basic form that deserves not to be forgotten.[8] However, when the re-writing of science textbooks was shown to be performing exactly the same function in Western society – of keeping memory of the past in alignment with the present state of scientific authority[9] – it seems probable that the Tiv demonstration was not known or profited from.

A major point needs to be made about this later fulfilment of Bartlett's programme: contrary to his expectation, the peoples whose time experience is posited as being structured by their social experience must be credited with an active role in the analysis. The clipping, elision and merging of sections of history is not something that is happening to them; it is something they are doing. They are very conscious agents. The Tiv who engage in disputes about political seniority derive some of their bargaining power from the numbers they can muster in support, and some from ancient genealogical right: at the end of the day, when settlement is reached, sheer numerical strength always wins over genealogy; consequently the genealogical charter has to be amended to fit the political reality that has been accepted. Their negotiating is from a short-term perspective. They do not have in mind the final resultant structure of their society. What they do with one set of purposes creates the unintended empty spaces or the thick clusters of fine discriminations that characterize their consciousness.

Beside the sophistication of this work, other generalizations about the experience of time seem childish indeed. The extreme methodological positivism, the search for objective bases for comparison, the trial and testing of data are recognizably in the tradition of the empirical sciences, as austere in what they do allow themselves to conclude as in that which is rejected as evidence.

Well before the self-fulfilling prophecy became a tag word in sociology, these self-limiting, self-validating processes of collective cognition were being analysed in the 1940s in greater intricacy than has since been achieved. Well before phenomenology's claim that sociological understanding must start from the negotiating activities of conscious, intelligent agents, Evans-Pritchard had seized the problem, developed a method and shown what progress can be made.

8. Nuer Religion

Now we come to Evans-Pritchard's book on *Nuer Religion*, the climax of the series that started with the promise that everyday knowledge should be compared with everyday knowledge, technology with technology, and theology with theology. At this point a shortcoming of the whole programme appears. When it was a matter of interpreting everyday meanings it was useful and necessary to remove artificial fences between primitive and modern thought. But when it comes to comparing theologies, the same boundaries may not be artificial. One explicit theology cannot be compared with another unless explicit theologizing is going on in both places. Evans-Pritchard started out with a wish to be led into alien worlds, to conduct his life by oracles if need be, to find meanings in the full context of actions. But in this final book he strait-jackets Nuer ideas by his own pre-formed judgement of what a book on religion should include. Nuer reflections on God, sin, sacrifice, spirit, symbolism are collected together for a moving theological statement.

Try to imagine a Nuer sage writing about Nuer religion; imagine him doing so without knowledge of the Western tradition and without intending to make Nuer experience accessible to Westerners. One should suppose he would plan his treatise very differently, choosing his key areas of exposition unpredictably, leaving major matters untouched, expatiating upon unexpected knotty problems. But there is no reason why a Nuer, living the life of a Nuer, should ever set about writing that book. The categories that give such treatises their life are the polemics of heterodoxy and orthodoxy. Neither is present in Nuer culture. The need to confound one's critics by theoretical synthesis belongs to a particular historical tradition.

If a great Talmudic scholar were to submit Nuer culture

to analysis, he would no doubt set it in a characteristic Talmudic perspective. If a learned Buddhist had thought of scrutinizing Nuer religious behaviour, he would fasten upon different elements. Presented by a Toltec priest or a Siberian shaman, each profound picture of Nuer religion would have been different. But the best interpretations would only fail to resemble the original in the minor ways that the Chinese painting entitled 'Cows in Derwentwater' does not immediately recall the English Lake District. Knobbly cows and trees stand in a Chinese style of landscape, but they are recognizably cows and trees; the lake, the misty mountain ridges are all there, checkable points of reference.[1]

Some writers belittle anthropological interpretation, maintaining that each effort betrays more of the contours of the translator's mind than of the original. I would argue that to dismiss attempts at translation because they do not correspond to an imaginary native text is a peculiar manifestation of Western thought. Eventually that Western desire for an impossible objectivity must lead the philosopher to the black edges of awareness. His pessimism about translation rests on a belief that he can never learn new things, only incorporate other people's experience within his usual categories. So he imagines interpretation as demanding an impossible leap from his own into another universe of thought.

A more modest programme is feasible if an attempt to interpret is seen as an enquiry within a conversation. The enquiry brings with it answers that change the next questions which can be asked. The enquirer's universe of knowledge itself is expansible. Evans-Pritchard adopted the task of explaining something important to his own generation. He determined that the proper method was comparative. For comparison between cultures, interpretation had to be tried. If he could alter the categories of his own generation's universe so that primitive peoples would rank in it as fully rational beings, that change would entail others, among them a higher status for religious knowledge in sociological thinking. His programme was to translate by selecting the key words and dominant themes or motifs. (Stated baldly, as he frequently stated it, there is nothing in that programme which guarantees that there will be checkable reference points from culture to culture.) He also insisted that crises of misfortune were the moments in which people revealed their central occupations so that the dominant themes could be recognized. To this rudimentary statement of his methodology I add that his actual analysis (as distinct from what he said he was doing) suggests a sound basis for translating and comparing cultures. In misfortune, people find ways of fixing accountability. Systems of accountability can be compared without departing from our steady foothold in our own scheme of knowledge, for they have checkable points of reference.

To treat alien theology as theology, Evans-Pritchard had to take theological scholarship seriously. He refreshed his knowledge of Greek philosophy, returned to the divinity books of his parsonage home, re-read the Bible, consulted Hebrew scholars, and generally ransacked the resources of his own culture to the best of his ability. It is as if no design would be grand enough unless it set Nuer thought accurately in the framework of Plato's vast polarities, illuminated with the sharp distinctions of the Desert fathers.

To give an idea of how wholeheartedly Evans-Pritchard entered upon the exegesis of Nuer religion, confident that it must yield its meaning to full and sensitive enquiry, I will introduce the themes of divine love, sacramental efficacy, and sin. The first, the assertion that the God of the Nuer can love, bore upon the contrary conviction, held by many missionaries, that primitive religion is based upon the emotion of fear. The second bore upon the widespread view that primitives performed magic instead of praying, expecting the rite to achieve results automatically. The third, the Nuer sense of merited punishment and their catalogue of sins, introduces the moral principles that explain the working of the feud and the automatic damper on political strife.

The book, *Nuer Religion*, starts with the conception of God. Immediately the flood of references to Hebrew and Greek ideas begins:

> The Nuer *kwoth*, like the Latin *spiritus*, the Greek *pneuma*, and the English derivatives of both words, suggests both the intangible quality of air and the breathing or blowing out of air. Like the Hebrew *ruah* it is an onomatope and denotes violent breathing out of air in contrast to ordinary breathing. In its verbal form it is used to describe such actions as blowing on the embers of a fire; blowing on food to cool it; blowing into the uterus of a cow, while a tulchan is propped up before it, to make it give milk; snorting; the blowing out of air by the puff fish; and the hooting by steam pressure of a river steamer. The word is also found, and has the same general sense, in some of the other Nilotic languages.
>
> As a noun, however, *kwoth* means only Spirit, and in the particular sense we are now discussing it means *kwoth nhial* or *kwoth a nhial*, Spirit of the heavens or Spirit who is in the heavens ...
>
> It would equally be a mistake to regard the association of God with the sky as pure metaphor, for though the sky is not God, and though God is everywhere, he is thought of as being particularly in the sky ...[2]

In this first chapter Evans-Pritchard sets out to show that the Nuer God is neither a thing of wood or stone, nor anthropomorphic, but a spiritual conception. God is in the sky, he is not the same as the sky, he is everywhere, he is especially in the sky as men are especially on the earth. He has no real physical location, no spatial boundaries. Thus the first big dichotomy is drawn between the things of above, associated with spirit, and the things of below, associated with men. But the divide is bridged: God intervenes in men's affairs; his lightning may strike and kill a person, whose spirit then is known as a child of God. Similarly, since divine intervention causes the birth of twins,

twins are known as children of God, and associated with high flying and migratory birds.

The first pages of Evans-Pritchard's exposition lay out the grounds for anticipating later chapters on spirits of the below, spirits of the sky, soul and ghost.

The Nuer extend their genealogical concepts to the physical universe and classify flora and fauna according to ascribed lineage relationships; it is not surprising that their conception of man's relations to God is in the model of human social relations. He is the father of men, he created them. Then the translation of the word to create has to be justified:

> God, Spirit in the heavens who is like wind and air, is the creator and mover of all things. Since he made the world he is addressed in prayers as *kwoth ghaua*, Spirit of the universe, with the sense of creator of the universe. The *cak*, used as a noun, can mean the creation, that is, all created things. As a verb 'to create' it signifies creation *ex nihilo*, and when speaking of things can therefore only be used of God. However, the word can be used of men for imaginative constructions, such as the thinking of a name to give a child, inventing a tale, or composing a poem, in the same figurative sense as when we say that an actor creates a part. The word therefore means not only creation from nothing but also creation by thought or imagination, so that 'God created the universe' has the sense of 'God thought of the universe' or 'God imagined the universe'.[3]

Adding together this with much more, the Nuer God is presented as creative spirit, a living person; he is ubiquitous and invisible, he sees and hears all that happens, and he can be angry and can love.

Here follows the deft aside: '(the Nuer word is *nhok*, and if we translate it "to love" it must be understood in the preferential sense of *agapo* or *diligo*: when Nuer say that God loves something, they mean he is partial to it).'[4]

But how does the anthropologist know that they mean *agapo* by a word that could be translated love? As in the case of the word create, the choice of *agapo* turns out to be very deliberate. Instead of only one chapter, half the entire book expounds the relationship between the individual Nuer and the Nuer God. Eventually love of a theologically recognizable kind dominates the relationship. It is not difficult to describe it, following Evans-Pritchard's method of collecting Nuer spoken prayers, their spontaneous references, their solemn invocations at final sacrifice; above all their attitude to misfortune, their trust and childlike confidence. Readers should place the reference to *agapo* in the context of all the possible relations between gods and their devotees. There are many religions known to history in which gods desire the sexual love of humans, charm, seduce, rape or otherwise take physical possession of them. There are religions also in which humans seek passionately for union with their gods and even achieve divinity for themselves. Fasting, vigils, feats of endurance and trance-inducing techniques compel the deity to reciprocate their longing.

The Lutheran theologian Anders Nygren recommended a method of comparing religions by what he called their fundamental motifs. Evans-Pritchard acknowledges Nygren[5] and was clearly influenced by him. It is worth placing side by side their remarks about method. Nygren traced the development of Christianity as a conflict between two concepts of love, the Hellenistic concept of *eros* and the novel Christian concept of *agape*, *eros* being the Platonic idea of motivated love, *agape* being self-giving, disinterested love given by God to his creatures. Justifying his focus on these themes, he said:

There is quite concrete proof of the existence both of another attitude to life of which the hallmark is *Eros*, and equally concrete proof of the existence of another attitude to life of which the hallmark is *Agape*, and these two general attitudes do not run side by side like parallel lines that never meet, but they constantly run into one another. At any point in the history of the spiritual life there is concrete evidence of a relation between them, inasmuch as each strives to put its stamp on the spiritual life as a whole. When we speak of *Eros* and *Agape*, therefore, we are thinking of them all the time in this sense – that is, as 'fundamental motifs' ... The term 'fundamental motif' requires more precise definition ... The most important task of these engaged in the more scientific study of religion and theological research is to reach an inner understanding of the different forms of religion in the light of their different fundamental motifs. For a long time they have been chiefly occupied in collecting a vast mass of material drawn from different religious sources for the purposes of comparison. But when the comparison actually comes to be made, the uncertainty of it immediately becomes apparent; for it is plain that no conclusion can be drawn from the mere fact that one and the same idea occurs in different religious contexts. The idea of belief may have exactly the same form without having at all the same meaning, if in one case it is a basic conception, while in another it is more loosely attached ... In other words we must try to see what is the basic idea or the driving power of the religion concerned, or what it is that gives it its character as a whole and communicates to all parts its special content and colour. It is the attempt to carry out such a structural analysis, whether in the matter of religion or elsewhere, that we describe as motif research.[6]

At the end of *Nuer Religion*, Evans-Pritchard wrote:

We have, therefore, in the study of primitive philosophies to begin anew to build up a theory and to formulate problems in the light of it. There is only one way in which this can be done. A number of systematic studies of primitive philosophies has to be made. When that has been done a classification can be made on the basis of which comparative studies can be undertaken which possibly may lead to some general conclusions ...

Such a classification of African philosophies must naturally be by reference to their chief and characteristic features. Among all African peoples we find in one form or another theistic beliefs, manistic cult, witchcraft notions, interdictions with supernatural sanctions, magical practices, &c., but the philosophy of each has its own special character in virtue of the way in which among that people these ideas are related to one another. It will be found that one or other belief, or set of beliefs, dominates the others and gives form, pattern, and colour to the whole. Thus, among some peoples, notably a large proportion of the Bantu, the dominant motif is provided by the cult of ancestors; among others, some of the Sudanic peoples for example, it is found in the notion of witchcraft, with which are bound up magical and oracular techniques; among others, such as the Nuer, Spirit is in the centre of the picture and manistic and witchcraft ideas are peripheral; and among other peoples yet other notions predominate. The test of what is the dominant motif is usually, perhaps always, to what a people attribute dangers and sickness and other misfortunes and what steps they take to avoid or eliminate them.[7]

According to Nygren, the first four centuries of Christian history had witnessed a new fundamental motif of religion and ethics, the *agape* motif struggled with the *nomos*, or legalistic motif of Judaism, and the spiritualizing, divinizing motif of *eros* in Greek religion, which allowed man to reach up to God and even aspire to divinity. The religions prior to Christianity extended to humans the possibility of deserving or attracting God's love, meriting it. The original Christian *agape* motif found all the initiative with God, rejecting the pride of man and the diminishing of Godhead implied by any doctrine of man's ability to reach upward. But by the end of the fourth century the *agape* motif was not dominant. Then Augustine developed a new synthesis, the *caritas* motif. This vigorous hybrid of love from God and love to God, according to Nygren, by dominating Catholic medieval theology allowed anthropocentric theories of merit and vainglorious works to creep back into a religion from which they had originally been rejected.

Under anthropocentric Nygren grouped all the religious motifs before and after *agape*, teaching that this distinctive theocentric motif was often threatened in the history of Christianity and even submerged. Luther 'discovered the *eros* feature of the *caritas*-synthesis. He therefore had to destroy it to make room for Christian love.'[8]

Nygren only used the contrast between anthropocentric and theocentric religions to clarify his reading of Christian church history. He did not pretend to offer any exhaustive typology for comparative religion. He wrote as the committed Lutheran expositor, the future President of the World Lutheran Foundation. Yet this simple typology is very rich and suggestive for comparative religion. Any doctrinal scope for laying love obligations on God implies fundamental adaptations in the rest of religious doctrine : God could have favourites; the unfavoured would fare less well in arbitrary judgements and distributions; doctrines of retribution would be revised away from universal categories; God's judgement might be misted by passion; the concept of law would be weaker; the whole universe would be seen differently. Especially would the response to misfortune be radically different, compared with a religion dominated by *agape*.

Evans-Pritchard did not try to make typologies, declaring the state of knowledge to be inadequate. When he says that Nuer attribute a selfless love to God, Nygren's interpretative framework is explicit.[9] Then for sure it becomes obvious, through everything the Nuer say and do about their wishes and misfortunes in daily life, that theirs is a theocentric religion and that *agape* is the closest word for *nhok*, when *nhok* is applied to God.

When there is a crisis and they do not know what to do, the Nuer comfort themselves saying God is present with them and will help them.[10] A ne'er-do-well asked how he

expected to live might reply : God is limitless (in his power
to aid).[11] The recital of their intimate, informal prayers and
their resignation in the face of adversity build up the theme
that they do not expect to sway him. God is always in the
right, the founder and guardian of morality. Up to a point
Nuer can avert trouble by behaving well. When the anthropologist was ill, they would come and say gently :

> 'Well, pray to God and tell him that you have come on a
> journey to the country of the Nuer and that you have
> not hit anyone or stolen anything or done any bad thing
> there, and then he will leave you alone'; or 'It is nothing.
> You will not die. This is our earth and you shall not die
> on it. Why should you die? You have not wronged us,
> and you are friend to all our children.' As these admo-
> nitions imply, if a man does wrong God will sooner or
> later punish him.[12]

But wrong-doing is not the only explanation for affliction.
God can do what he likes with his own.

> Nuer accept misfortunes with resignation. Whatever
> the occasion of death and other misfortunes may be,
> whether they be what Nuer call *dung cak*, the lot of
> created things, or whether they be the result of what
> they call *ducri*, faults, they come to one and all alike,
> and Nuer say that they must be accepted as the will of
> God ... When a child dies women lament, but only for a
> little while, and men are silent. They say that God has
> taken his own and that they must not complain; perhaps
> he will give them another child ... Likewise if a cow or
> an ox of your herd dies Nuer say that you must not com-
> plain if God takes his own beast. The cattle of your herd
> are his and not yours. If you grieve overmuch God will
> be angry that you resent his taking what is his. Better be
> content, therefore, that God should do what he wishes,
> seeing not that he has taken one of your cows but that
> he has spared the others. If you forget the cow God will

see that you are poor and will spare you and your children and your other beasts. I cannot convey the Nuer attitude better than by quoting the *Book of Job*: 'the Lord gave, and the Lord hath taken away; blessed be the name of the Lord' (1. 21).[18]

Many more passages show the Nuer admitting their feebleness, smallness, stupidity before God. This is in striking contrast to their overbearing pride before any other humans. Before God they are like ants, so small, like idiots, so simple-minded.

Nygren showed great insight when he clustered together characteristic Lutheran Christian forms at one pole of the historical comparison, calling them theocentric, in contrast with anthropocentric religions. Sure enough, the Nuer sense of the chasm between godhead and created things entails several other ideas that link to make the predicted pattern. Nuer passivity in the face of misfortune that they could not attribute to human responsibility was complementary to their pugnacity in all other cases. Their resignation when God was seen to have intervened was as brave as their resistance to damage caused by another person. The two kinds of accountability supported each other by their grounding in the concept of 'being in the right'. A man knew when he was in the right in any human transaction because kinsmen showed that they agreed, by fighting with him. Their mutual liabilities being precisely detailed and put to the test, uncertainty was reduced. But this was not possible in relation with God, for God always had the right on his side. Being in the right was a much more central idea to this cosmology than loving. Yet, as its implications unfold, Nygren's predicted correlatives of a religion based on a particular doctrine of love and responsibility emerge. If Evans-Pritchard wanted to interpret an exotic religion in a way that would be intelligible within the Judeo-Christian tradition, he could hardly do better than present Nygren's thesis.

One bias in Nuer behaviour is especially significant for

comparison with Christian doctrinal history: their empha-
sis on intention in the justification of man before God. Right
intention as distinct from right ritual focused the bitterest
controversies of the Reformation and remains the most frequently used of Christian religious typologies. On the one
hand, a trend to formalism, the preference for prescribed
performance of ritual, on the other a preference for spontaneity, sincerity, directness: formalism places value on
public worship, spontaneity prefers private worship. The
advocates of spontaneity will tend to treat intention as the
only effective means of attracting God's aid, while the advocates of formalism will tend to prescribe efficacious rites.
When efficacy can be attributed to actions and things, the
way is open for commerce in them. One point of view
entails another and another until the initial contrast takes
us all the way back to Luther's attack on clerical corrup-
tion, simony, and the sales of indulgences. It also embraces
the difference between prayer and magic; Reformation
apologetics associated Protestantism with prayer and
Catholicism with magic so explicitly that five centuries
later Robertson Smith could draw up a plausible scale of
moral evolution showing Catholicism and other magic-
ridden religions being outdistanced by more ethical, spiritual
forms of belief.[14]

Taking God to be the guardian of the moral order, the
Nuer believed him to be more concerned with intention
than with action, as were they themselves in their dealings
with one another. They paid less compensation for killing a
man by a fishing spear or a club than with a fighting spear,
for it was less likely to have been premeditated:[15]

When I was living on the Sobat river news came to our
village that some persons in an upstream village had
found some meat and had cooked and eaten it, thinking
that it was the flesh of some animal crocodiles had mutilated, and that they had later discovered it to be the
flesh of a man whom crocodiles had killed and torn to
pieces. I was told that these persons would at once have

taken *wal nueera*, medicine to cleanse them from pollution, and that while the happening was very disgusting it was unlikely that it would cause death because the flesh was eaten in ignorance of its nature. Nuer say that God may overlook what was done in error. Similarly, they say that he will not allow a curse to harm a man who has done no deliberate wrong.[16]

There is still a sense in which a wrong act is always a wrong act whether deliberate or not. In their accounting with each other, the Nuer have a fair chance of winning because they all know the rules. But in their accounting with God, the ambiguities and possible consequences overwhelm the case they might like to make. Between man and God, man cannot win, even by the most scrupulous observance of the moral law, for human faults are inevitable and accumulate. In the end God's adverse judgement will catch up with them. The same for sacrifice, the high moment in man's relation with God : it is not a magical act designed to produce prosperity. Three chapters in Evans-Pritchard's book explain it as the central framework of their relation to God, expressing everything they know, their identification with cattle, with kin, their knowledge of sin, their trust and faith. On all the important points, the Nuer would be aligned with Protestants and advanced religion. This should have come as a great surprise to professors of comparative religion, and if he had known about it, would have been a real problem for Nygren's thesis that the *agape* motif was unique to Christianity.

Since I do not intend to follow his entire book through its analysis of soul, ghost, totems and spear symbolism, I may diverge from its path to mention that sacrificing cattle is one of the ways that the Nuer put pressure on each other and recognize claims. If one pays attention through the book to the Nuer occasions of sacrifice, one recognizes trails cut by relations travelling from far to attend this funeral or that purification or peace-making. In this way kinship claims are made evident at sacrificial rites, by the ostentatious effort of traipsing across the country to be there. Religion provides another medium in which people confront one another and require that deeds support sentiments. Presence at sacrifices constitutes kinship and is part of the legitimating background for claims to cattle or wives. Religion, then, is a double set of accounts: it enables people to hold each other accountable to a common commitment to rituals which testify to their right-mindedness; it also provides a balance sheet on which their relation to God can be assessed.

It is true Nuer do not take a formalistic magical approach to get the prosperity they desire, but when it comes to reckoning the causes of disaster, they are very precise and formal. Each class of sin is tallied against a class of illness which it will cause. Enteritis is a sign of one kind of offence, eczema another, backache another. No matter what the cause, the cure is always a sacrifice. And here the casuistic grading of big and little offences adjusts the gravity of sins to the value of the beast to be offered. God, being just and all-knowing, will even accept a wild cucumber in token sacrifice for an ox promised for later. But the spirits are greedy and less considerate. A man may be forced to drive hard bargains with them. The owner of a herd of cattle has to meet several different kinds of claims against them: first, the claim of his dependants to have milk to drink; second, the demand to kill livestock to pay héavenly debts; and third, the demand to let them be driven away in payment of social debts.

If a man refused to pay up in the social transactions, the whole system would collapse like a pack of cards. It is no small political achievement that any Nuer to whom a cow is owing can go and collect his debt in a camp of strangers with all the immunities of law. The pressure of cattle debts being strong, the wish to evade payment must be strong also. The possibility of fighting it out when one has had the misfortune to kill another must be more attractive than paying over full forty head of cattle. However, the social debts tend to get paid, within geographical and social limits. As we have seen, these payments create communities which recognize their own distinct identity and are able to ally with neighbours to defend their rights against more distant foes. But the regular fission and fusion which bring strife to a truce when balanced segments confront each other depends on the imbalance in transactions between God and man.

God's being heavily in the right allows the Nuer to set a limit to claims. Radiating out from anyone's homestead, there are borderline conflicts where the limit to claims has been reached. Men may not lay all their sorrows to the door of fellow men. God is responsible for the most grievous. Or rather, they accept that their disasters are God's penalties on them for acts for which they are responsible. There is a limit to claiming and blaming. The friends of an afflicted man press him to accept his troubles as coming from God. No one can claim redress for hidden psychic sources of damage; no searching of oracles to know who is bewitching sick children or casting a murrain on the cow. Accepting God's judicial interventions, accepting themselves as always in the wrong in his sight, means a limit to claims.

Further, all the rules of a self-equilibrating system of vengeance and self-help work homeostatically because God makes rightful claims. Making themselves responsible to God, they make God ultimately responsible. In many political systems based on self-help, vendetta killing escalates indefinitely. Nuer can force each other to settle their feuds with fixed transfers of cattle, because human affairs are never capable of balancing out with God. Like playing a game in which the dealer is always bound to win: the stakes may as well be lowered because no one is going to win against God. The heavy debt in the divine accountability enables the other set of accounts to balance out. The rates at which human accountability is reckoned can be settled arbitrarily by conventions unquestioningly applied. The accumulated debt to God is a kind of cushion that absorbs the unaccountable shocks from social life. God takes a long time to make good his claims, but in the end, his justice catches up with the most secret defaulter. Since God is on the side of right, he is the collector of debts for those who cannot do so for themselves, and the thought of his heavy-handed intervention encourages payment. It is as if his eye for detail were extremely sharp: he even notes the origin of cattle in a homestead: if a woman for whose marriage they have been paid, or a wronged husband to whom they came in compensation for adultery, were to drink milk of the cows, sickness will befall. God does not cause it directly, but has set up the retributive universe. By requiring respect for cows given for different particular purposes, God's universe requires the Nuer to respect those purposes. He even punishes a man who fails to respect his in-laws by appearing improperly dressed in their presence. Collecting dues in the form of sickness and expiatory sacrifice for neglecting these intimate forms of respect, God upholds the moral law where no human has a private claim. He causes mortal sickness for a whole community when homicide among its members makes it likely that the kin of the slayer and kin of the victim drink the same water. Here he is collecting a claim that no one in the community can collect, since the feud would normally divide it into two internecine camps. When he punishes an incestuous couple, he upholds the principle by which everyone else regulates their accounts, namely that 'where the women are, the cattle are not', based on the rule that one person cannot both give cattle and receive cattle in the same situation. When he punishes adultery by afflicting an injured husband with backache, he might seem to be acting arbitrarily: the innocent party, not the guilty pair bears the penalty. But no: the universe is not siding with lovers. Whether the husband knows or does not know about the adultery, his lethal backache makes him a victim of his wife's seducer; if he were to die the adulterer will be forced by the rest of the community to pay the full blood compensation for taking a life. This belief is as good a way as any that has been devised for flushing out the secret adulterer, forcing him to confess and pay for the sacrifice lest the husband's illness worsen and a suit for adultery turn into a suit for homicide.

So one way or another each of the peculiar beliefs in the causes of illness fit together like a key in a lock. There is nothing unusual in itself in finding that God is collecting uncollectable claims on behalf of the wider community, or helping disadvantaged persons, wives, in-laws, cuckolds, to collect on their own behalf. Recalling the neurological model I mentioned in Chapter 1, the Nuer God's righteousness irresistibly suggests Sherrington's distance perceptor – a delayed and sustained attention, stabilizing the organism as a whole. Evans-Pritchard had no trouble in resisting the mechanistic analogy. Yet I am sure that I have not over-systematized his thinking here. His style in *Nuer Religion*, while leisurely in quoting Nuer remarks, is terse in commentary upon them. The system appears in the way he constructed the trilogy. The first two books are especially condensed. To make the tight construction easier I have had to labour clumsily at pointing out connections between them and the third.

By the time that Evans-Pritchard finished his book on Nuer religion his initial programme was complete. He had worked through the exercises required to establish a distinctive anthropological theory of knowledge. He could demonstrate the reasonableness of what seemed to be the wild flights of fancy, unbridled fears, haphazard mental associations, and mystic participations that were supposed to govern primitive thought. He first dismantled the imaginary constructs of earlier thinkers. He had to extract each piece of primitive theorizing, clean it and get it into working order, then set it carefully back into its functioning context. He had to restore to their institutional setting thoughts that only seemed like nonsense because they had been abstracted and put into a false context. His own objective was clear and limited. He would not have dreamed of devaluing scientific knowledge. His frequent references to reality and objectivity made it clear that he accepted the views current in his own society about the nature of the world as it is. These views were neither his target, nor something he was trying to defend. His readership would certainly have taken him for a lunatic if he adopted a relativist view, negating the possibility of comparing the values of kinds of knowledge. His target was within epistemology, and not concerned with the science of being. Consequently he assumed, from his declared standpoint, that the Azande were wrong about witchcraft and the Europeans were right. He would have lacked credibility if he had asked his colleagues to credit the Azande theory that a witch can leave his body sleeping in his bed and fly through the air to a midnight necrophagous rendezvous, or any other such ideas from the history of witchcraft. To have raised the mere possibility that these ideas provided explanations of illness as sound as those found in our current state of medical knowledge, would have roused the same intelligent opposition then as it would today. His strictures against earlier writers for their gross misunderstanding of primitive religions may have seemed to imply that they would have done better if they had been believers themselves instead of agnostics or atheists. But he is against that view. The anthropologist does not have to have a religion of his own.[17] The only mistake would be to carry forward into his interpretation of foreign beliefs any strong hostility or deep disagreement with religious believers from his own culture. Not being a theologian he is not concerned with the truth of religious ideas. A negative theological view, imported at the outset, to the effect that their religion is false, would be as damaging to the anthropological enquiry as a negative judgement passed prematurely on the value of their agricultural techniques or an unqualified positive evaluation of their medicine.

Primitive mentality had created a problem in psychology because the primitive was clearly wrong about witches, ghosts and zombies, and consistently wrong in very interesting ways. Evans-Pritchard's answer was to change the direction of enquiry away from objective rightness and wrongness, and away from psychology towards sociology and the workability of a system of ideas. He tried to focus the discussion upon the service that theories afford for ordinary life. His approach was the consequence of a theoretical position stemming from the assumptions of the French sociologists who had first posed the problems in this form. They lacked empirical procedures. He proposed to test and develop their ideas by methodically tracking each verbal statement to its context of action and, ultimately, to its place in a coherent system of accountability.

Evans-Pritchard's method provides non-arbitrary criteria for considering meaning. When he taught that anthropology was more akin to history than to science[18] he was not denying the need for objectivity or the need for classification and systematic comparison. He was asking that fieldworkers be equipped with the insights of the historian's discipline. A good example of the scientific theorizing that he repudiated, and which is still in disrepute, comes from Professor C. G. Seligman's Foreword to *Witchcraft among the Azande*. It is generous, witty and urbane. But at one or two points we get a glimpse of what the book might have been like in other hands: 'The Zande, as it seems, retains his infantile aggressive instincts through life, but unlike so many savages, he does not project these on to a more or less well-defined high God or on to the spirits of his ancestors.'[19] Seligman also mentions introversion, normally associated with religion; extraversion, in this case associated with magic, animism, and he says that 'something perhaps comparable to the "censor" of Freud has come into existence and inhibited what we should call the common sense of the belief.' At least Seligman credited the belief with common sense, but by other writers it could easily have been endowed with more anthropomorphic features and be set to play within some mechanical theory to attack, counteract, neutralize or inhibit other beliefs.

By avoiding such conceits, beloved in the 1930s or 1940s, Evans-Pritchard stands clear of current criticisms of psychological theorizing. Consider a modern effort to disengage the insights of psychoanalysis from the distortions of functional analysis based on biological models. Roy Schafer argues that intentionality and personal meaning, the constituents of psychic reality and therefore the essential matter of psychoanalysis, are arbitrarily thinned and narrowed, reduced and even excluded by the technical language of functions and energies; this is especially so for the concept of meaning.[20] Schafer's own preferred language for recasting the general theory so that it fits clinical practice is that of history. Evans-Pritchard also called to his aid the trained historical imagination. In the same spirit, he was inveighing against reductionist theories of religion. Sociological analysis was necessary, but wrong if it taught that the religious conceptions of primitive peoples were nothing more than symbolic representations of the social order.[21] What the person says the gods and spirits mean to him is as irreducible a datum as his statements about economic choice.

The collective expression of religion has to be distinguished from the personal; from the first we learn more about the social order, from the second we learn what religion is. The Nuer conception of God cannot be reduced to or explained by the social order. When all the purely social and cultural forms have been abstracted, what is left is a description of a relationship between man and God. It transcends all forms, so not surprisingly the Nuer cannot tell us what is the nature of this spiritual relationship.[22]

Nothing can take us beyond the verbal metaphors on the one hand and the pledges of conviction on the other. We can understand the metaphors insofar as we have a common experience over which translation is possible. But meanings will never yield to functional analysis. For Evans-Pritchard the anthropologist's task is to trace meanings, but not to pronounce them right or wrong.

9. Contradiction

Anyone reading the preceding chapter may be struck by a contradiction: Evans-Pritchard's concern was to lower the artificial partitions between kinds of thought, especially primitive and modern; at the same time he recognized a difference between philosophizing and everyday thought. Here, evidently, are partitions he thought useful. In order to do justice to the philosophical depths of Nuer religious thought he had to dig up terms from old Christian controversies and contrast *agape* with *eros* in the senses used by Nygren. But the sharp-eyed critic will recall that the theologian had based his typology of religions on one kind of legalism, *nomos*, and three kinds of love, *agape*, *eros* and *caritas*. Evans-Pritchard never mentioned the possibility of the Nuer religion being based on *caritas* or on *nomos*. But why not? Evidently the match that he discerned between Lutheran and Nuer conceptions of grace and godhead were so striking that it was enough of an argument to state them.[1] If the critic concedes that major point, there are still other difficulties in his text not to be summarily dismissed. Surely it goes against his own principles to take the words of another civilization and use them to make distinctions or to cover up contradictions which are not observed in the culture being interpreted. Here we are deep into anthropology's most difficult problems about translation, and close to those original questions about the thought processes of Indians who declare that they are birds and apparently accept such simple self-contradiction as true.

Evans-Pritchard dealt with apparent contradictions in different ways. The Nuer statement that human twins are birds he treated as an example of analogical thinking. Because they are in the same class as birds, when Nuer twins die they are not buried but their corpses are laid across the forks of trees. Evans-Pritchard explained the classification by depicting the general structure of Nuer analogies by which God is to men as the sky above is to the earth below, as birds are to land animals. The migratory birds that fly up and away, without being seen to land, are especially like spirits, close to God. Humans usually give birth to young singly; two births are a sign of divine intervention, so twins are to ordinary mortals as birds are to animals, close to God, a manifestation of spirit.

Among the Azande beliefs, he discovered some implicit contradictions by tracing different lines of argument back to statements that would be seen as contradictory if Azande ever were to make them explicit, but which represented assumptions belonging to clearly segregated institutions which would never be brought into conflict in the ordinary Azande experience. This corresponds to the bounding of curiosity as Bartlett described it. The incoherence detected in their thought is systematically related to the interlocking of their institutions.

A third way of dealing with apparent contradiction is to pursue the path of correct translation. It would be tempting to hope that with these three solutions, metaphor, separation of spheres of life, and good translation, all the apparent nonsenses of primitive thought could be interpreted as sense at one level or another. But the more conscientious the translation, the more a new problem about contradiction arises. It is probably wise for the ethnographer faced by paradox or contradiction to assume that by the end of the day, when he knows all the sentences held by the natives to be true, they will be found to make a coherent scheme. But the next example suggests that the assumption of ultimate coherence may be wrong.

Evans-Pritchard tried to decide whether Nuer religion was really monotheistic or polytheistic. When he saw a major contradiction, I believe he chose the wrong way to interpret it, importing a concept even more foreign and specialized than *agape* to bridge the gap.

It would be too simple to conclude, from the fact that they speak of gods in the plural, that the Nuer are polytheists. For one thing, Nuer insist that there is only one God.[2] But is the term 'god' quite right for the idea? Evans-Pritchard could ask the question, 'Do you believe in one god or in many?' but his rules of method forbade him to rely on their verbal answer to a verbal question. He had to observe that the singular and plural forms were used in different contexts. The question then turned on a difference of practice. When the Nuer used the singular form, the context refers to creator, father, judge, owner, great spirit in heaven; while the plural form always refers to spirits of the air and to other spirits tied to particular places or lineages. God in the singular is the same great spirit for everyone, but these spirits in the plural have different importance for different people. Spirits in the plural may pass in and out of families, be remembered and forgotten, possess someone, make another sick, or otherwise make claims to respect. When a Nuer falls ill, if they cannot establish another cause, his relatives may get a prophet or diviner to examine the victim's family history or discover whether a forebear might not have had a spirit whom they have neglected.

After considering in detail all the contexts of sacrifice, consecration of cattle to spirits, and rite of exorcism, Evans-Pritchard tells us that there is no question of Nuer regarding these spirits as beings of the same importance as God. 'Whatever else they may be thought to be, they are not thought of as beings independent of and equal to him. There is only one God.'[3] Among the facts he cited in evidence are the following linguistic usages. As they have no proper name for God, the Nuer cannot easily distinguish their God from the God of another people; though aware of their neighbours' differing religious beliefs, they regard them all as communicating with the same God as theirs, only under different titles. Apart from spirits attached to lineages and families, they also believe in spirits of the heavens. Any of these can be referred to individually, as a spirit but never as *the* spirit of heaven, that is, God. Referring to an individual spirit of heaven as relatively great compared with lesser ones, they can say: '*a* great spirit,' never 'the great spirit'. The difference turns decisively on the use of the definite article. The Nuer call the spirits of the air children of God, to denote their lesser status below the Father-God in the sky. They could be translated as godlings, angels, demons. The Nuer attitude to the spirits is as towards mischievous beings, exacting and jealous. God is above the capricious, greedy behaviour they are credited with. The final test appears in the way the Nuer settle accounts with spirits : 'in making amends through sacrifice a bargain is struck in a much cruder and more human way than when a sacrifice is made to God. The Nuer will bargain with a spirit, trying to buy it off as cheaply as he can, but never with God, and no Nuer would use such familiar terms in addressing God as he sometimes uses in addressing spirits.'[4] The Nuer hold themselves accountable to God in a more serious way than their accountability to spirits. On these lines the case against their polytheism is sustained : there is one Nuer God and the other spirits are different and lesser.

At this point everything would be quite simple and straightforward, if only according to Nuer statements the spirits of the air were not also God; they are many and also one. The Nuer see no contradiction, so presumably their scrupulous ethnographer should not find a difficulty in passing as they do 'from a more general and comprehensive way of conceiving God or Spirit to a more particular and limited way of conceiving God or Spirit, and back again. This is often very apparent in invocations made at their sacrifices and in what they say in times of sickness and other troubles. Therefore a question which tries to present a disjunction, an either ... or, in answer to which either one proposition or the other may be accepted but not both, is not understood.'[5] This problem is very different from the relation of analogy which holds between spirits and birds, twins and humans, so that twins are as birds. To translate the identity and difference that affects the relation between the many spirits and the one God Evans-Pritchard resorted to calling the spirits manifestations of God, local refractions of godhead. He also used the word hypostasis.

The philosopher W. V. Quine has suggested that 'wanton translation can make the natives sound as queer as one pleases. Better translation imposes our logic upon them.'[6] He has also entered the caveat that the further we get off home ground the less sense there is in saying what is good translation or bad. Without a basis of comparison between two kinds of historical experience, there is little basis for translation. He gives as an example of this problem a little point of criticism made by Edmund Leach in elucidating some statements by Malinowski. Quine adds generously: 'It is understandable that the further alternative of blaming the translation of conjunctions, copulas or other logical particles is nowhere considered; for any considerable complexity on the part of the English correlates of such words would of course present the working translator with forbidding practical difficulties.'[7] So it is worth recording that Evans-Pritchard was exceptional in not shirking these forbidding difficulties. As well as faithfully watching for the difference between a spirit and the spirit, Evans-Pritchard also scrupulously scouted out the verb to be, separating the senses of to exist, to be in the same class as, to be the same as. None of this helped him when the Nuer affirmed that the spirits were different from God and at the same time one with God. Spirits of the air, he said, 'are not thought of as independent gods, but in some way as hypostases of the modes and attributes of a single God.'[8] Hypostasis is a theological term meaning person of the godhead. If it were the correct term in this case, the spirits would not behave differently from God, capriciously or greedily, but as one person. We have the interesting case of a wrong term being introduced to resolve a contradiction that might worry us, did originally worry our own theologians, but that did not worry the Nuer. It was unnecessary to translate their thought by a term that had no equivalent in their language. The tolerance of one and many as noncontradictory or a mystery is common to many religions at different levels – Islam, Buddhism, and popular Christianity. In Christian cultic practice not only God, but also the Virgin Mary is seen as one and many : as one historical person, efficacious in prayer, she is also manifest in numerous shrines and statues each having different material efficacies, god-like but more human than God and not above demanding special attention and exacting small revenges. The same meticulous labours of interpretation bestowed on the Spanish, Irish, Italian Catholics, would reveal their godlike pantheons of powerful archangels and saints. One upshot of the exercise is to make these words 'polytheism' or 'monotheism' not be lightly used, so immense the labour of ethnography that goes into determining their sense. Another upshot is to show the deformation of thought that is risked by the interpreter who is determined to make everything somehow translatable.

We feel a very different mood pervade Dr R. G. Lienhardt's book on Dinka thought. Lienhardt, a close friend and associate of Evans-Pritchard, went in 1947 to study these neighbours of the Nuer. Seen from the Nuer viewpoint, the Dinka appeared in *Nuer Religion* as more magic-minded. When Evans-Pritchard reported mechanical approaches to God, divination and fetishes among the Nuer, he always noted that they were said to be of recent origin, imported from the Dinka. The Nuer individual's habit of praying to God out loud when in trouble occasioned much surprise among the Dinka. One way and another, *Nuer Religion* leads us to expect the Dinka religion to be more materialistic, more fetishist than Nuer forms of spirituality.

Evans-Pritchard would have been disappointed if Lienhardt's Dinka study had slavishly followed the lines of his own, but no danger of that. Here is an anthropologist, profiting from the earlier work, avoiding its mistakes, and leaning over backwards not to impose his own logic. Lienhardt starts by explaining why he prefers not to use the word God at all. Divinity with a capital for the central concept of immanent creator, and divinity writ small for the lesser manifestations. He does not address the set of questions normally associated with theology. Every page of his book shows how inappropriate and misleading it would be to carve an old-fashioned, strictly theological topic out of the lives of people whose whole consciousness is informed by the experience of divinity. He broadens his focus to the fundamental questions in the psychology of perception: not merely how misfortune is perceived, as Evans-Pritchard taught, but even how space and colour are perceived. Ultimately, I suppose, Lienhardt's book approaches the old question of how magic gets credence. But the method assumes a total suspension of belief, going beyond the credibility of magic to the point at which it can be asked how anything is credible, ever. Why does anyone ever consent to any version of reality? The answer comes in the many-tiered levels of sense that public rituals affirm. Liturgy endows action with meanings; the received meanings define perceptions and enclose interpretations.

This treatment does not need archaic medieval terminology to reveal the philosophical depth and subtlety of Dinka thought. By unpressured advance from interpreting very simple acts (the herdmen's knotting of a twist of grass to delay supper till his return) to violent sacrificial killings (the red ox that symbolizes the main divinity, Flesh) and emotive scenes of burial alive (the famous priest insisting on his right to be placed dying in his grave, his last breath to be kept in his body for a final benefit to his community). Perhaps the most extraordinary analysis is of this divinity, Flesh, and its hereditary priests. Whereas lesser divinities are manifested in different animal or other emblems, Flesh is the life in the living being. It is the divinity of cool judgement, clear light, truth, discernment. Its worshippers feel it stirring in their bodies, making them tremble and fall into ecstatic trance when invocations are chanted.

The divinity Flesh has as its emblems real flesh and blood, primarily in the bodies of men, the masters of the fishing-spear. There is a ceremony for 'feeding' the Flesh in their bodies, though I have never seen it. It is said that

E-P.–E

at certain sacrifices to the divinity Flesh, which unlike other sacrifices take place at night, masters of the fishing-spear take small pieces of raw flesh from the victim and eat them with great solemnity before day breaks.* A master of the fishing-spear of the clan Paghol, which has the primacy in the Apuk Patuan tribe of the Rek, said that he would very respectfully take three small pieces of raw flesh from the thigh of an ox sacrificed for Flesh,† and would eat them to feed (augment) the Flesh ...

... They are observances connected exclusively with masters of the fishing-spear, and they set them apart from others in sharing a mystery which others do not share. It is said that the 'red' beasts sacrificed for the divinity Flesh are to be consumed utterly by the elders of their community in a byre at night, after the sacrifice. This is the only case of a solemn eating of the clan-divinity.

*Cf. W. Robertson Smith, Lectures on the Religion of the Semites, *note to p. 221 of the 1907 edition: '... certain Saracen sacrifices, nearly akin to the Passover, which were even eaten raw, and had to be entirely consumed before the sun rose. In this case the idea was that the efficacy of the sacrifice lay in the living flesh and blood of the victim. Everything of the nature of putrefaction was therefore to be avoided ...'*

†*Thigh and Thigh-bone is the principal divinity of this clan.*[9]

This passage illustrates the temptations resisted. Lienhardt relegated the Passover parallel to a footnote citing Robertson Smith; the Christian Eucharistic parallels are not mentioned at all. On the one hand Lienhardt's field research does not seek to reveal an accountability system or base an articulated system of thought upon a system of social action. However, on the other hand, the Dinka ethnography is a better fulfilment of Evans-Pritchard's project than subsequent studies of religion, which were more reductionist and less attentive to philosophical insights. Earlier, I compared Evans-Pritchard's idea of understanding language always in its practical functions with Wittgenstein's comparison of language with an instruction manual. It would sadly miss the mark if this approach implied that language in action could not open out to embrace all human intuitions and syntheses, if it could not make poetry as well as build ships.

One way to assess Evans-Pritchard's achievement is to see how many old questions have been laid to rest and new ones are now in play. The difference between a systematized dogmatic theology and the theological constructions of everyday life are now much clearer. The idea that there will be no contradictions in everyday thinking has been tried and rejected. Furthermore contradictions at the level of everyday thinking are no longer a sign of intellectual weakness. Lienhardt's development from Evans-Pritchard's work leads us to expect insoluble antimonies to arise at deep levels of enquiry. The ship-building manual would have to be consistent throughout, but one would expect metaphysical assumptions inevitably to involve contradiction if transferred to superficial levels of explanation. At more profound depths of understanding large incompatible assumptions about life and death and truth may be held together in unresolved conflict to fulfil the interpretive requirements of human society.

10. Evans-Pritchard's Contemporary Influence

The concluding chapter is the place to check earlier statements that may seem too sweeping or tendentious. It has not been difficult to place Evans-Pritchard in relation to his predecessors, they having earned their clearer outline by the passage of time: compared with the poetic speculations of Marrett or Frazer or with the rigid scheme of Lévy-Bruhl, or with Bartlett's failure to develop a sociological theory of perception, or Haddon's theory of conventionalizing, Evans-Pritchard seems to speak to us with the lonely voice of common sense. But if this story were only to record the victory of plain thinking over theorizing, it would be a dull tale and discouraging to theorists. For common sense is prejudiced and hasty in judgement. It is not likely to be always right, and it cannot take the place of theoretical method. However, when we try to compare Evans-Pritchard with his own contemporaries assessment of his work becomes more worthwhile – though much more difficult. We must start by separating off as not strictly relevant the work of those of his generation who had no special interest in the theory of knowledge or in any problems of human cognition. Though this seems arbitrarily to exclude a number of important contemporaries whose concern lay with political science or economics, Evans-Pritchard himself did some such bracketing off from his own concerns when he listed the large number of studies in anthropology that did not attempt to contribute directly to the understanding of thought systems.[1]

I should mention some apparently relevant movements in cultural analysis in the United States. From the beginning of this century two common ideas in philosophical commentary have found a sympathetic and quasi-technical niche in anthropology: one is the assumption of cultural holism, the other the separation of culture from behaviour.

The first gave rise to easy writing about world views, cultural patterns, central motifs, dominant themes, configurations of culture. The second allowed these latter to be considered as autonomous or at least as capable of being analysed independently of social organization.[2]

None of the practitioners of cultural analysis developed a method for relating the levels of behaviour which their initial assumptions had split apart, nor for overcoming the temptation to compose wholes out of a quick subjective intuition about how the elements of a culture seem to cohere. Writing about culture, Evans-Pritchard was concerned to find an objective method of justifying his own interpretation. As I have reiterated, the method was to trace the discriminations that are made by people holding one another accountable. This includes stewardship over material possessions and all other moral justifications. This method set a new standard for fieldwork which vaguer formulations of the problem did not require, and provoked new specialized kinds of enquiry. So though they seem relevant, the work of anthropologists on the American side of the Atlantic in the 1930s and 1940s went in a different direction and addressed different problems.

The same can be said of a postwar generation of anthropologists whose reaction against the looser style of their seniors in cultural anthropology created ethno-science and cognitive anthropology. These sub-specialities are indeed sensitive to the problem of subjective bias and good translation. To meet the challenge of interpretation over exotic areas, they select a set of coordinates common to each language, and use componential analysis to identify areas of overlapping or divergent meaning within a micro-scale domain.[3] But a convincing passage from this degree of accuracy to full-scale ethnography has never been demonstrated. The methods and intentions are so much closer to those of linguistics that it is safe to exclude these scientists from a record of those whose work is close to that of Evans-Pritchard.

Among British anthropologists it is difficult to separate

the various strands of their interests. Many were close collaborators, interested in the same problems and themselves also all influenced by Radcliffe-Brown, Malinowski and the French sociologists. For example, one of the closest colleagues is Meyer Fortes, whose original work on personal identity and on filial relations uses the same general principles of validation.[4] It is a fully independent corpus, its roots in psychoanalytic theory, its materials from west Africa, its style of questioning and testing all its own. Yet the effect of having grown alongside the growth of Evans-Pritchard's work is undeniable. Comparisons of different kinds of blame-pinning which culminate in sorcery and witchcraft accusations proved a rich seam in African ethnography in the 1950s and 1960s, taking the insights of the Azande study to more dynamic styles of political analysis.[5] A host of concerns which have radiated out from shared work include comparisons of local theories of personality and their accompanying variations in social experience,[6] sociological perspectives on religious conversion,[7] and on types of acceptable explanation.[8] Comparative religious studies have been influenced by interpretations of spirit possession[9] and of ancestral cults,[10] analysis of the social and political differences likely to be found with variant forms of monotheism[11] and the everyday role of ritual in shaping cognized reality.[12] It must also be important to record Evans-Pritchard's profound influence on a generation of Oxford historians.[13]

I should also mention Evans-Pritchard's encouragement to a new young field of Mediterranean anthropology[14] and his influence on Islamic studies.[15] At the same time he was encouraging Rodney Needham's translations of the French thinkers of the *L'Année Sociologique* group, and overseeing with Godfrey Lienhardt the scholarly publication by the Clarendon Press of African texts side by side with English translations.

At this close focus upon such a large collaboration it is impossible to give definition to the distinctive work of scholars who were his friends and who influenced him as well as he influenced them. Since a man is partly to be judged by his friends, the confused attribution is a part of the picture. In the era of postwar expansion, British anthropologists had become much more professional than their immediate prewar predecessors and more sociologically inclined in their outlook than American contemporaries. They shared ideas and argued vehemently in that close atmosphere of competitive scholarship which is splendid for beating definitions into shape, though less well adapted for spreading a message beyond the ranks of the initiated.

After this over-view of detailed interactions, it is necessary to paint with the big brush. In this past quarter century three outstanding names represent the world's most famous work on human thinking processes: Piaget on learning, Lévi-Strauss on culture, Noam Chomsky on language. Their work represents three developments from the ideas about primitive mentality, of the early decades of this century. Chomsky attends to the innate capabilities of the human mind, Piaget to its developmental process. Both are interested in phylogenetic questions – how the human faculties are organized and what the limits to their capabilities may be; both implicitly expect their questions to lead back to the physiology of the brain. Clearly the direction they follow is very different from the researches just outlined. Much closer is Lévi-Strauss's chosen path, for while he, too, is interested in the innate structure of the human mind, he traces the relation between forms of rationality and social factors, and takes problems about primitive modes of classification seriously. If I may indulge in the privilege of posterity, I would simplify by saying that he illuminates the paradoxes of totemism in two grand moves. First he puts an end to separate enquiries about itemized peculiarities of totemic belief, requiring it rather to be set out on the larger canvas of all analogic thinking about classes of humans and classes of animals. Primitive thought, he argues, is dominated not by the means-end chain of inference that leads to work, but by a controlled exercise in metaphorical construction. He develops and popularizes a method of structural analysis that makes sense of what once seemed nonsense, the sense of analogy in place of the nonsense of contradiction. Although he works in the recalcitrant materials of ethnography, his method applies to any literary work of art. By virtue of his own command of matter and style, he fuses together what had, since Frazer's decline, become two separate fields, civilized literature and primitive mythology. Second, he neither began nor rested with a demonstration of the literary and philosophical power of mythological imagery. Originally he developed a typology of kinship and marriage and always sought to relate it to totemic and other modes of thought. Against the dazzle of his success, the contribution of his contemporaries must seem to pale. But what he has achieved only takes us a certain way along the path of understanding human cognitive powers. His work, highly schematic and typological, is based on an inadequate basis of information. This means that he is tempted to brandish his grand generalizations prematurely. Lévi-Strauss never leaves any mystery unsolved. His method for analysing complex structures of contrast and similarity applies to anything and everything. It never fails. A method adapted from linguistic and literary analysis, it appears to be much more than a mere method, because its application to esoteric and ancient myths enters a claim to unveil the hidden movement of our prehistoric consciousness. Since it draws a special appeal from this claim to interpret primitive thought,[16] he keeps alive the practical dichotomy which assigns anthropology to the shallows and purlieus of philosophy.

To conclude this side of the comparison between his work and Evans-Pritchard's, it is important to recognize that his is a different programme of enquiry from that which took its roots in William James's interest in mental associations, in Frederick Bartlett's concern with memory, and in Marcel Mauss's questions about the socializing of the physical body. The latter asked about how incoming sensory data are screened and organized, how memory functions, what selective principles of attention are at work and the social factors that enter into the cognitive process. Though Lévi-Strauss has offered some ideas on these topics[17] they are not central to his main interests and influence.

These cursory remarks drawn in light and dark are intended to sharpen the contrast with Evans-Pritchard, to show up the strengths and weaknesses of each. The Englishman was wary of grand intellectual schemes, careful to a point of scrupulosity about correct translation. His strength was in fieldwork, his weakness in schematic ordering. This very weakness came from a personal scepticism about the possibility of objective knowledge and thence from an unusual sophistication on epistemological matters. By comparison, Lévi-Strauss often seems to walk in eighteenth-century innocence. For him data is data, however gathered : when he discovers error, he corrects his theories and realigns his scheme, but his greatness in interpretive synthesis is not matched by sensitivity to problems about subjective awareness. So the two great contemporary anthropologists, with all due respect for each other, were following different lights, attracted to different problems and working in different ways.

Evans-Pritchard's implicit conception of human knowledge starts from three principles. First, rational thought is exercised only selectively over the possible field of attention. Second, the principles of selectivity depend upon the social demand for accountability. Third, the social patterns of accountability which can be elicited by systematic observation provide a structured anchorage for a particular kind of reality, with its own array of beings invested with appropriate powers. In sum, each human society, insofar as its members expect to hold each other accountable, has its own locally selected reality anchored to a literary and impressionist stage of research. The anthropologist should

discover the structural order of the society, so that it is intelligible not merely at the level of consciousness and action, as it is to one of its members or to the foreigner who has learnt its mores and participated in its life, but also at the level of sociological analysis. Just as the linguist does not merely seek to understand, speak and translate a native language but seeks to reveal its phonological and grammatical systems, so the social anthropologist is not content merely to observe and describe the social life of a primitive people but seeks to reveal its underlying structural order, the patterns which, once established, enable him to see it as a whole, as a set of interrelated abstractions.[18]

Having identified these structural patterns in one society, the social anthropologist is expected to compare them with patterns in other societies. I said above that Evans-Pritchard was guided by a feeling for epistemological directness. When he wrote about beliefs and meanings he assumed straightforwardly that a statement would only be counted as a belief if actions were regularly observed to be consistent with its truth. His teaching implied that a consensual commitment to a way of life is inherently a commitment to a way of thought and vice versa. Michael Polanyi,[19] who was much influenced by Evans-Pritchard's Azande study, was one of the few in England at that time to be interested in what he called the fiduciary element, or the element of commitment and trust, in any knowledge. Now that the air has cleared and now that philosophers have worked through the pitfalls of earlier controversies, Evans-Pritchard emerges from the past as if he had, impossibly, been reared in a modern theory of knowledge. I would say not that he was saved by luck, or made modern by the turn of the wheel, but that he was legitimately ahead of the game because of a powerful insight and patient reasoning.

He had worked out how to relate sentences to beliefs with maximum confidence, checking to see how much the speakers staked upon what they said. From this securer basis in comparative accountability, we note that different accounting systems would call forth different arrays of hard physical facts. By emphasizing this use of accountability as a common area of human experience on which to base common understanding and safer interpretation, I exaggerate any claim to a special methodology he would have been prepared to make. Evans-Pritchard was not too modest to claim methodological insights. He was too sceptical at too fundamental a personal level to seek or claim security in knowledge. He did not think the problems are easy or that any guarantees of truth can be trusted.

> We feel like spectators at a shadow show watching insubstantial shadows on the screen. There is nothing Nuer can say of the nature of God or other spirits than that he is like the wind or air ...[20]

> A study of the symbols tells us nothing of the nature of what is symbolized. Spirit in itself is for the Nuer a mystery which lies behind the names and the totemic and other appearances in which it is represented ...
> Words and gestures transport us to a realm of experience when what the eye sees and the ear hears is not the same as what the mind perceives. Hands are raised in supplication to the sky, but the sky is not being supplicated.[21]

The ancestor's antique spear is really a new spear recently bought from an Arab trader. Or the ancestral spear is non-existent, a man making gestures with it by moving his empty hand as if the spear were there. The sacrificial ox stands for the sacrifice, but the sacrificer may not be present at all; even the ox may be represented by a cucumber.

> We seem indeed to be watching a play or to be listening to someone's account of what he has dreamt. Perhaps when we have this illusion we are beginning to understand, for the significance of the objects, actions and events lies not in themselves, but in what they mean to those who experience them as participants or assistants ... when we reflect on their meaning we perceive they are a dramatic representation of a spiritual experience.[22]

Given this profound philosophical doubt and given that his ways of dealing with it were provisional suspensions or containments, what right have I to claim that his attention to misfortune is a methodologically central tool? None, no right, but I have good reasons for drawing attention to the resounding implications of his usage. At this time, younger anthropologists, beset by philosophical quandaries from which they see no escape, are content to treat the best understanding they can report as well-observed, deeply interpreted fictional texts.[23] Evans-Pritchard's descriptions also probe contradictory statements and reveal the delicate strain and balance between desires. For such penetrating sensitivity he was once described as the Stendhal of anthropology. But he showed the way to do something different from fiction. By systematically attending to people's response to misfortune, he justified the distinctive claims of his chosen profession.

Notes

1. Introduction

1. 'Genesis of a Social Anthropologist', p. 18.
2. See Gregory Bateson, *Naven*, p. 292.

2. Human Mental Faculties

1. B. Von den Steinen, 'Unter der Naturvolken Zentral-Brasiliens'.
2. L. Lévy-Bruhl, *How Natives Think*, p. 62.
3. See J. C. Crocker, 'My Brother the Parrot', p. 165. See also G. Van der Leeuw, *La Structure de la mentalité primitive*, p. 8; R. Lowie, *History of Ethnological Theory*, p. 218; W. Percy, 'The Symbolic Structure of Interpersonal Process'; L. Vygotsky, *Thought and Language*, p. 71; C. Geertz, 'Religion as a Cultural System', pp. 37–8; and J. Z. Smith, 'I am a Parrot (Red)'.
4. R. K. Merton, 'The Sociology of Knowledge'.
5. R. K. Merton, 'Karl Mannheim and the Sociology of Knowledge', p. 544.
6. L. Lévy-Bruhl, 'A Letter to E. E. Evans-Pritchard'. See Evans-Pritchard's note on the letter to him from Lévy-Bruhl.
7. See R. Otto, *The Idea of the Holy* (also A. Lang, quoted in E. Sharpe, *Comparative Religion: a History*, p. 61).
8. See S. F. Nadel, 'Malinowski on Magic and Religion', p. 195.
9. C. Elliot Smith, *In the Beginning*.
10. 'Genesis of a Social Anthropologist', p. 19.
11. G. Ferrero, quoted in A. C. Haddon, *Evolution in Art*, pp. 300–1.
12. F. C. Bartlett, *Thinking*, p. 142.

125

13. ibid., p. 143.
14. F. C. Bartlett, *Psychology and Primitive Culture*, p. 63.
15. ibid., p. 110.
16. ibid., pp. 117–18.
17. F. C. Bartlett, *Thinking*, p. 144.
18. See F. C. Bartlett, *Psychology and Primitive Culture*, ch. 4.
19. M. Mauss, 'Les Techniques du corps'.
20. M. Halbwachs, 'La Mémoire collective chez Les Musiciens'.
21. F. C. Bartlett, *Remembering*.

3. The Continuity of Evans-Pritchard's Programme

1. 'Lévy-Bruhl's Theory of Primitive Mentality', p. 29.
2. ibid., pp. 28–9.
3. 'Science and Sentiment', p. 184.
4. idem.
5. ibid., p. 185.
6. See B. Malinowski, *Coral Gardens and their Magic*, vol. II.
7. 'Lévy-Bruhl's Theory of Primitive Mentality', p. 3.
8. ibid., pp. 8–10.
9. 'Science and Sentiment', p. 188.
10. 'The Intellectualist (English) Interpretation of Magic', p. 311.
11. L. Wittgenstein, *Philosophical Investigations*, paras 23, 11, 12, 19.
12. ibid., paras 325, 326.
13. ibid., para. 132.
14. ibid., para. 125.

4. Fieldwork Methods

1. See H. Balfour, *Spinners and Weavers in Anthropological Research*.

2. *Social Anthropology*, p. 72.
3. See F. Boas, 'The Study of Geography'.
4. See C. G. Seligman and B. Seligman, *Pagan Tribes of the Nilotic Sudan*.
5. See R. Firth, ed., *Man and Culture: an Evaluation of the Work of Bronislaw Malinowski*.
6. *Social Anthropology*, p. 74.
7. ibid., pp. 78–9.
8. Quoted as dedication to A. Singer and B. V. Street, eds., *Zande Themes: Essays Presented to Sir Edward Evans-Pritchard*.
9. *Witchcraft, Oracles and Magic among the Azande*, p. 220.
10. *The Nuer*, pp. 8–9.
11. *Nuer Religion*, p. ix.
12. *The Nuer*, pp. 14–15.
13. 'Some Aspects of Marriage and Family among the Nuer'.
14. See 'Fragment of an Autobiography', p. 37.
15. See 'Genesis of a Social Anthropologist', p. 18.
16. See G. Lienhardt, 'E.P.: a Personal View', p. 304.
17. *The Sanusi of Cyrenaica*, p. 2.

5. Accountability among the Azande

1. J. L. Austin, *How to Do Things with Words*.
2. A. Cicourel, *Cognitive Sociology*, p. 112.
3. M. Polanyi, *Personal Knowledge*, pp. 287–94; P. Winch, 'Understanding a Primitive Society'; H. F. Pitkin. *Wittgenstein and Justice*, pp. 247–50.

6. Accountability among the Nuer

1. *The Nuer*, pp. 151–2.
2. ibid., p. 142.
3. ibid., p. 157.
4. ibid., pp. 157–8.

5. ibid., p. 158.
6. ibid., pp. 181–2.
7. ibid., p. 229.
8. ibid., pp. 205, 211, 212, 228, 229, 236; *Kinship and Marriage among the Nuer*, pp. 179, 180.

7. Reasoning and Memory

1. F. C. Bartlett, *Thinking*, pp. 142–4.
2. F. C. Bartlett, *Remembering*, p. 222.
3. M. Halbwachs, *Les Cadres socèaux de la mèmoire*.
4. F. C. Bartlett, *Remembering*, pp. 279–81.
5. *The Nuer*, pp. 34–5.
6. *Kinship and Marriage among the Nuer*, ch. 2.
7. *The Nuer*, p. 108.
8. L. Bohannan, 'A Genealogical Charter'; J. A. Barnes, *Politics in a Changing Society*; I. G. Cunnison, *The Luapula Peoples of Northern Rhodesia*; R. F. Murphy, 'Tuary Kinship'.
9. T. S. Kuhn, *The Structure of Scientific Revolutions*.

8. Nuer Religion

1. Wash and ink (1936), reproduced in E. H. Gombrich, *Art and Illusion*, p. 84.
2. *Nuer Religion*, pp. 1–2.
3. ibid., pp. 4–5.
4. ibid., p. 7.
5. *Essays in Social Anthropology*, p. 54; *Theories of Primitive Religion*, p. 14.
6. A. Nygren, *Agape and Eros*, p. 35.
7. *Nuer Religion*, p. 315.
8. A. Nygren, *Agape and Eros*, p. 72.
9. *Theories of Primitive Religion*, p. 14; *Essays in Social Anthropology*, p. 54; *Nuer Religion*, p. 317.
10. *Nuer Religion*, p. 9.

11. ibid., p. 4.
12. ibid., p. 17.
13. ibid., p. 12.
14. W. Robertson Smith, *The Religion of the Semites*.
15. *Nuer Religion*, p. 107.
16. ibid., pp. 17–18.
17. *Theories of Primitive Religion*, p. 17.
18. *Social Anthropology*, p. 60.
19. *Witchcraft, Oracles and Magic among the Azande*, p. xviii.
20. R. Schafer, *A New Language for Psychoanalysis*, pp. 93–6.
21. *Nuer Religion*, p. 313.
22. ibid., p. 321.

9. Contradiction

1. *Nuer Religion*, pp. 317–18.
2. ibid., p. 48.
3. idem.
4. ibid., p. 51.
5. ibid., pp. 51–2.
6. W. V. Quine, *Word and Object*, p. 58.
7. idem; E. R. Leach, 'The Epistemological Background to Malinowski's Empiricism', p. 130.
8. *Nuer Religion*, pp. 49, 117.
9. G. Lienhardt, *Divinity and Experience*, pp. 143–4.

10. Evans-Pritchard's Contemporary Influence

1. *Theories of Primitive Religion*, pp. 112–13.
2. A good short account of the problems of investigating culture in this sense of shared meanings cut off from shared economy and shared politics is given by Zygmunt Bauman, *Culture as Praxis*.
3. S. A. Tyler, 'Introduction'.

4. M. Fortes, *Oedipus and Job in West African Religion*. This work has its own large bibliography of criticism, controversy and development.

5. J. C. Mitchell, *The Yao Village*; M. G. Marwick, *Sorcery in its Social Setting*; I. Schapera, *Rainmaking Rites of Tswana Tribes*; J. Middleton and E. H. Winter, eds., *Witchcraft and Sorcery in East Africa*; M. Douglas, ed., *Witchcraft Accusations and Confessions*; V. W. Turner, *Schism and Continuity in an African Society*.

6. R. Horton, 'Destiny and the Unconscious in West Africa'.

7. R. Horton, 'African Conversion' and 'On the Rationality of Conversion'.

8. R. Horton, 'African Traditional Thought and Western Science'.

9. P. Fry, *Spirits of Protest*; I. I. Zaretsky and C. Shambaugh, eds., *Spirit Possession and Spirit Mediumship in Africa and Afro-America*; J. Beattie and J. Middleton, eds., *Spirit Mediumship and Society in Africa*; E. Colson, 'Spirit Possession among the Tonga of Zambia'; I. M. Lewis, *Ecstatic Religion*.

10. J. Middleton, *Lugbara Religion*; T. O. Beidelman, 'The Ox and Nuer Sacrifice'.

11. B. C. Ray, *African Religions*.

12. J. Buxton, *Religion and Healing in Mandari*; Beidelman, 'Some Nuer Notions of Nakedness, Nudity and Sexuality'.

13. K. Thomas, 'Should Historians be Anthropologists?'

14. J. G. Peristiany, *Honour and Shame*; J. Pitt-Rivers, *The People of the Sierra*; J. Davis, *People of the Mediterranean*.

15. E. L. Peters, 'The Proliferation of Segments in the Lineage of the Bedouin of Cyrenaica'; E. Gellner, *Saints of the Atlas*; I. A. Lewis, *A Pastoral Democracy*; A. P. Stirling, *Turkish Village*; S. M. Salim, *Marsh Dwellers of the Euphrates Delta*.

16. C. Lévi-Strauss, *La Pensée sauvage*.

17. ibid.

18. *Social Anthropology*, pp. 61–2.
19. M. Polanyi, *Personal Knowledge*, pp. 287–94.
20. *Nuer Religion*, p. 321.
21. idem.
22. ibid., p. 322.
23. C. Geertz, *The Interpretation of Cultures* and 'Found in Translation'.

Short Bibliography

Evans-Pritchard's Writings

1933 'The intellectualist (English) interpretation of magic'. *Bulletin of the Faculty of Arts* (Egyptian University, Cairo), I, 282–311.

1934 'Lévy-Bruhl's Theory of Primitive Mentality'. *Bulletin of the Faculty of Arts* (Cairo), II, 1–36.

1936 'Science and Sentiment: an Exposition and Criticism of the Writings of Pareto'. *Bulletin of the Faculty of Arts* (Cairo), Part 2, 163–92.

1937 *Witchcraft, Oracles and Magic among the Azande.* Oxford: the Clarendon Press.

1938 'Some Aspects of Marriage and Family among the Nuer'. *Zeitschrift fur vergleichende Rechtswissenschaft*, LII, 306–92.

1940 *The Nuer: a Description of the Modes of Livelihood and Political Institutions of the Nilotic People.* Oxford: the Clarendon Press.

1948 'Social Anthropology: an Inaugural Address delivered before the University of Oxford on 4 February 1948'. Oxford: the Clarendon Press.

1949 *The Sanusi of Cyrenaica.* Oxford: the Clarendon Press.

1950 'Social Anthropology: Past and Present' (The Marett Lecture). *Man*, L (Sept.), no. 198, 118–24.

1951 *Social Anthropology* (The Broadcast Lectures). London: Cohen and West.

1951 *Kinship and Marriage among the Nuer.* Oxford: the Clarendon Press.

1956 *Nuer Religion.* Oxford: the Clarendon Press.

1962 *Essays in Social Anthropology.* London: Faber and Faber.

1965 *Theories of Primitive Religion.* Oxford University Press.

1973 'Genesis of a Social Anthropologist'. *New Diffusionist*, vol. 3, no. 10 (January), 17–23.
1973 'Fragments of an Autobiography'. *New Blackfriars* (January), 35–7.
1980 *A History of Anthropological Thought*. London: Faber and Faber.

Other Works

Austin, J. L., *How to Do Things with Words*. Oxford: the Clarendon Press, 1962.
Balfour, H., *Spinners and Weavers in Anthropological Research*. Oxford: the Clarendon Press, 1938.
Barnes, J. A., *Politics in a Changing Society*. Manchester: University of Manchester Press, 1967.
Bartlett, F. C., *Psychology and Primitive Culture*. Cambridge: Cambridge University Press, 1923.
Bartlett, F. C., *Remembering: a Study in Experimental and Social Psychology*. Cambridge: Cambridge University Press, 1932.
Bartlett, F. C., *Thinking: an Experimental and Social Study*. New York: Basic Books, 1958.
Bateson, G., *Naven* (second edition). Palo Alto: Stanford University Press, 1958.
Bauman, Z., *Culture as Praxis*. London: Routledge and Kegan Paul, 1973.
Beattie, J., and Middleton, J., eds, *Spirit Mediumship and Society in Africa*. London: Routledge and Kegan Paul, 1969.
Beidelman, T. O., 'The Ox and Nuer Sacrifice: Some Freudian Hypotheses about Nuer Symbolism'. *Man*, I, 4 (1966), 453–67.
Beidelman, T. O., 'Some Nuer Notions of Nakedness, Nudity, and Sexuality'. *Africa*, XXXVIII, 2 (1968), 113–32.
Boas, F., 'The Study of Geography'. *Race, Language, and Culture*, 639–47; New York: Macmillan, 1887.

Bohannan, L., 'A Genealogical Charter'. Africa, XXII, 4 (1952), 301–15.

Buxton, J., *Religion and Healing in Mandari*. Oxford: the Clarendon Press, 1973.

Cicourel, A., *Cognitive Sociology*. Harmondsworth: Penguin Books, 1973.

Colson, E., 'Spirit Possession Among the Tonga of Zambia'. *Spirit Mediumship and Society in Africa*, 69–103; London: Routledge and Kegan Paul, 1969.

Crocker, J. C., 'My Brother the Parrot'. *The Social Use of Metaphor: Essays on the Anthropology of Rhetoric*, ed. D. Sapir & C. Crocker, 164–92; University of Pennsylvania Press, 1977.

Cunnison, I. G., *The Luapula Peoples of Northern Rhodesia*. Manchester: Manchester University Press, 1959.

Davidson, D., 'On the Very Idea of a Conceptual Scheme'. *American Philosophical Association Proceeding and Addresses*, XLVII (1973), 5–21.

Davis, J., *People of the Mediterranean*. London: Routledge and Kegan Paul, 1977.

Douglas, M., ed., *Witchcraft Accusations and Confessions*. London: Tavistock Publications (ASA, 9), 1970.

Dumont, L., 'Preface' to *Les Nuers*. Paris: Editions Gallimard (I–XV), 1968.

Ferrero, G., *Les Lois Symboliques du Symbolisme*. Reference *Haddon*: 300–1.

Firth, R., ed., *Man and Culture: an Evaluation of the Work of Bronislaw Malinowski*. London: Routledge and Kegan Paul, 1957.

Fortes, M., *Oedipus and Job in West African Religion*. Cambridge: Cambridge University Press, 1959.

Fortes, M., 'Pietas in Ancestor Worship'. *Journal of the Royal Anthropological Institute*, XCI, 2 (1961), 166–91.

Fortes, M., 'La Notion de Personne en Afrique Noire'. *Collogues Internationaux du Centre National de la Recherche Scientifique*, 544 (1971), 283–319.

Fortes, M., 'Custom and Conscience in Anthropological Perspective'. *International Review of Psychoanalysis*, IV (1977), 127–54.

Foucault, M., 'L'Ordre du Discours'. *Archéologie du Savoir*; Paris: Gallimard, 1964.

Frazer, J. G., *The Golden Bough*. London: Macmillan, 1911 (third edition).

Fry, P., *Spirits of Protest*. Cambridge: Cambridge University Press, 1976.

Geertz, C., 'Religion as a Cultural System'. *Anthropological Approaches to the Study of Religion*, 37–8; London: Tavistock Publications (ASA, 3), 1966.

Geertz, C., *The Interpretation of Cultures*. New York: Basic Books, 1973.

Geertz, C., 'Found in Translation: on the Social History of the Modern Imagination'. *Georgia Review*, XXXI, 4 (1977), 788–810.

Gellner, E., *Saints of the Atlas*. London: Weidenfeld and Nicolson, 1969.

Gombrich, E. H., *Art and Illusion*. Princeton: Princeton University Press, 1972 (paperback).

Haddon, A. C., *The Decorative Art of New Guinea: a Study in Papuan Ethnography*. Dublin: the Academic House, 1894.

Haddon, A. C., *Evolution in Art as Illustrated by the Life Histories of Designs*. London: Scott, 1895.

Halbwachs, M., *Les Cadres sociaux de la mèmoire*. Paris: Alcan, 1925.

Halbwachs, M., 'La Mémoire collective chez Les Musiciens'. *Revue Philosophique* (1939), 136–65.

Halbwachs, M., *La Morphologie Sociale*. Paris: A Colin, 1970 (originally 1938).

Halbwachs, M., *La Mémoire collective*. Paris: Presses Universitaires de France, 1950.

Horton, R., 'Destiny and the Unconscious in West Africa'. *Africa*, XXXI, 2 (1961), 110–16.

Horton, R., 'African Traditional Thought and Western Science'. *Africa*, XXXVII, I (1967), 50–71 (Part I), and 2 (1967), 155–87 (Part II).

Horton, R., 'Types of Spirit Possession in Kalabari Religion'. *Spirit Mediumship and Society in Africa*, 14–49; London: Routledge and Kegan Paul, 1967.

Horton, R., 'African Conversion'. *Africa*, XLI, 2 (1971), 85–108.

Horton, R., 'On the Rationality of Conversion'. *Africa*, XLV, 3 (1975), 219–35 (Part I), and 4 (1975), 373–99 (Part II).

Kuhn, T. S., *The Structure of Scientific Revolutions*. Chicago: University of Chicago Press, 1962.

Leach, E. R., 'The Epistemological Background to Malinowski's Empiricism'. *Man and Culture: An Evaluation of the Work of Bronislaw Malinowski*, 119–37; London: Routledge and Kegan Paul, 1957.

Lévi-Strauss, C., *La Pensée sauvage*. Paris: Plan, 1962.

Lévy-Bruhl, L., 'A Letter to E. E. Evans-Pritchard'. *British Journal Sociology*, III, 2 (1952), 117–23.

Lévy-Bruhl, L., *How Natives Think* (*Les Fonctions mentales dans les sociétés inférieures*: Paris, 1910). NY: Washington Square Press, 1966.

Lewis, I. M., *A Pastoral Democracy*. London: Oxford University Press for the International African Institute, 1961.

Lewis, I. M., *Ecstatic Religion*. Harmondsworth: Penguin Books, 1971.

Lienhardt, G., *Divinity and Experience; The Religion of the Dinka*. Oxford: the Clarendon Press, 1961.

Lienhardt, G., 'E.P.: A Personal View'. *Man* (n.s.), 9 (1974), 299–304.

Lang, A., *The Making of Religion*. London: Longmans, Green, 1900 (second edition).

Lowie, R., *History of Ethnological Theory*. New York: Farrar and Rinehart, 1937.

Malinowski, B., *Coral Gardens and their Magic*, vol. II. London: Allen and Unwin, 1935.

Marwick, M. G., *Sorcery in its Social Setting: a Study of the North Rhodesian Cewa*. Manchester: Manchester University Press, 1965.

Mauss, M., 'Les Techniques du corps'. *Journal du Psychologie*, 3–4, extract in *Sociologie et Anthropologie*; 365–86;

Paris: Presses Universitaires de France, 1936.

Merton, R. K., 'Karl Mannheim and the Sociology of Knowledge'. *Social Theory and Social Structure*, 543–62; New York: Free Press, 1941 (enlarged edition).

Merton, R. K., 'The Sociology of Knowledge'. *Social Theory and Social Structure*, 543–62; New York: Free Press, 1945 (enlarged edition).

Middleton, J., *Lugbara Religion*. London: Oxford University Press for the International African Institute, 1960.

Middleton, J. and Winter, E. H., eds, *Witchcraft and Sorcery in East Africa*. London: Routledge and Kegan Paul, 1963.

Mitchell, J. C., *The Yao Village*. Manchester: Manchester University Press, 1956.

Murphy, R. F., 'Tuary Kinship'. *American Anthropologist*, 69 (1967), 167–70.

Nadel, S. F., 'Malinowski on Magic and Religion'. *Man and Culture: an Evaluation of the Work of Bronislaw Malinowski*, 195; London: Routledge and Kegan Paul, 1957.

Nygren, A., *Agape and Eros*. New York: Harper and Row, 1969 (originally *Eros och Agape*; Stockholm, I and II, 1936).

Otto, R., *The Idea of the Holy*. London: Oxford University Press, 1917 (English translation).

Percy, W., 'The Symbolic Structure of Interpersonal Process'. *Psychiatry* 24 (1961), 39–52.

Peristiany, J. G., *Honour and Shame: the Values of Mediterranean Society*. London: Weidenfeld and Nicolson, 1965.

Peters, E. L., 'The Proliferation of Segments in the Lineage of the Bedouin of Cyrenaica'. *Journal of the Royal Anthropological Institute of Great Britain and Ireland*, 90 (1960), 29–53.

Pitkin, H. F., *Wittgenstein and Justice*. Berkeley and Los Angeles: University of California Press, 1973.

Pitt-Rivers, J., *The People of the Sierra*. Chicago: University of Chicago Press, 1961.

Polanyi, M., *Personal Knowledge*. London: Routledge and Kegan Paul, 1973.

Quine, W. V., *Word and Object*. Cambridge, Mass.: the MIT Press, 1960.

Radcliffe-Brown, A. R., *The Andaman Islanders*. Cambridge: Cambridge University Press, 1933.

Ray, B. C., *African Religions: Symbol, Ritual and Community*. Englewood Cliffs: Prentice Hall, 1976.

Rignano, E., *The Psychology of Reasoning*. London: Routledge and Kegan Paul, 1920.

Salim, S. M., *Marsh Dwellers of the Euphrates Delta*. London: Athlone Press, 1962.

Schafer, R., *A New Language for Psychoanalysis*. New Haven: Yale University Press, 1976.

Schapera, I., *Rainmaking Rites of Tswana Tribes*. Cambridge: African Studies Centre, 1971.

Seligman, C. G. and Seligman, B., *Pagan Tribes of the Nilotic Sudan*. London: G. Routledge and Son, 1932.

Sharpe, E., *Comparative Religion: A History*. London: Duckworth, 1975.

Sherrington, C. S., *Man on His Nature*. Cambridge: Cambridge University Press, 1953 (second edition).

Singer, A., and Street, B. V., eds, *Zande Themes: Essays Presented to Sir Edward Evans-Pritchard*. Oxford: Basil Blackwell, 1972.

Smith, C. Elliot, *In the Beginning: the Origin of Civilization*. New York: Morrow, 1928.

Smith, J. Z., 'I am a Parrot (Red)'. *History of Religions*, II (1972), 391–413.

Smith, W. Robertson, *The Religion of the Semites: the Fundamental Institutions*. New York: Schocken Books, 1972.

Stirling, A. P., *Turkish Village*. London: Weidenfeld and Nicolson, 1965.

Thomas, K., 'Should Historians be Anthropologists?' *Oxford Magazine*, (1961), 387–8.

Turner, V. W., *Schism and Continuity in an African Society: a Study of Ndembu Village Life*. Manchester: Manchester University Press, 1957.

Tyler, S. A., 'Introduction'. *Cognitive Anthropology*, 1–27;

New York: Holt, Rinehart and Winston, 1969.

Van der Leeuw, G., *La Structure de la mentalité primitive*. Paris: 1928.

Von den Steinen, K., *Unter der Naturvolken Zentral – Brasiliens*. Berlin: Verlagsbuklandlub Dietrich Reimer, 1894.

Vygotsky, L., *Thought and Language*. Cambridge: the MIT Press, 1962.

Wiener, N., *Cybernetics*. New York: Wiley, 1948.

Winch, P., 'Understanding A Primitive Society'. *American Philosophical Quarterly*, I (1964), 307–24.

Wittgenstein, L. (trans. G. E. M. Anscombe), *Philosophical Investigations*. Oxford: Basil Blackwell, 1972.

Zaretsky, I. I. and Shambaugh, C., eds, *Spirit Possession and Spirit Mediumship in Africa and Afro-America: an Annotated Bibliography*. New York and London: Garland Publishing, Inc., 1978.

Lévi-Strauss
Edmund Leach

The theories of Claude Lévi-Strauss aim at no less than an understanding of the human mind. They combine, to quote the author of this book, 'baffling complexity' with 'overwhelming erudition'. In unravelling the complexities, Dr. Leach balances a sharply critical approach to his subject with a generous recognition of its importance, and he combines erudition with consideration for the layman.

'Leach, the analytic anthropologist, faults many of Lévi-Strauss's basic purposes—for example, the attempt to establish facts 'universally true of the human mind'. But Leach rightly admires Lévi-Strauss's remarkably revealing handling of complex traditions, and so attempts only to curtail Lévi-Strauss's extravagance.' *The Birmingham Post*

'Dr. Leach, with great good humour and impartiality, explains Lévi-Strauss's originality, castigates his intellectual arrogance and theoretical dogmatism, and puts him into perspective not only within the field of anthropology, but also in the general history of thought.'
John Weightman, *The Observer*

Fontana Paperbacks

Fontana is a leading paperback publisher of fiction and non-fiction, with authors ranging from Alistair MacLean, Agatha Christie and Desmond Bagley to Solzhenitsyn and Pasternak, from Gerald Durrell and Joy Adamson to the famous Modern Masters series.

In addition to a wide-ranging collection of internationally popular writers of fiction, Fontana also has an outstanding reputation for history, natural history, military history, psychology, psychiatry, politics, economics, religion and the social sciences.

All Fontana books are available at your bookshop or newsagent; or can be ordered direct. Just fill in the form and list the titles you want.

FONTANA BOOKS, Cash Sales Department, G.P.O. Box 29, Douglas, Isle of Man, British Isles. Please send purchase price, plus 8p per book. Customers outside the U.K. send purchase price, plus 10p per book. Cheque, postal or money order. No currency.

NAME (Block letters)

ADDRESS
